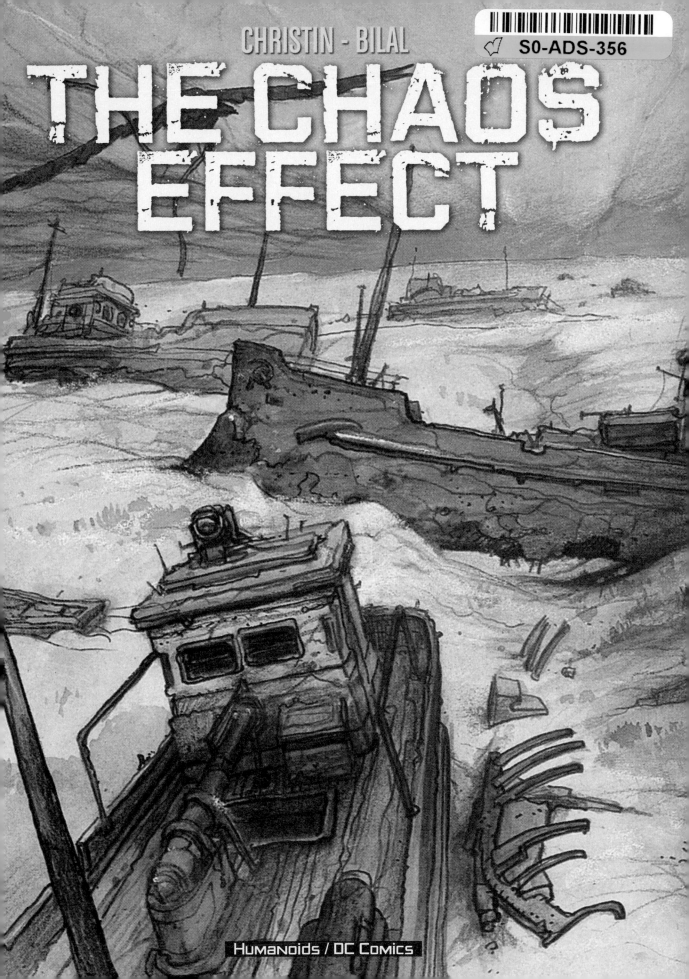

CHRISTIN - BILAL

THE CHAOS EFFECT

Humanoids / DC Comics

"The sleep of reason breeds monsters."
–GOYA

PIERRE CHRISTIN, Writer
ENKI BILAL, Artist
JUSTIN KELLY, Translator

THIERRY FRISSEN, BOOK DESIGNER
PATRICK LEHANCE, LETTERER
FRANCIS LOMBARD, EDITOR, COLLECTED EDITION
MAXIMILIEN CHAILLEUX & FABRICE GIGER, EDITORS,
ORIGINAL EDITION

THE CHAOS EFFECT, Humanoids Publishing. PO Box 931658, Hollywood, CA 90094. This is a publication of DC Comics, 1700 Broadway, New York, NY 10019.

The Chaos Effect and The Chaos Effect logo and Humanoids, are trademarks of Les Humanoides Associes S.A., Geneva (Switzerland). DC Comics is ® DC Comics. English version is copyright © 2005 Humanoids, Inc., Los Angeles (USA). All rights reserved. Humanoids Publishing is a division of Humanoids Group. DC Comics is a Warner Bros. Entertainment Company. No portion of this book may be reproduced, by any means, without the express written consent of Humanoids Publishing. Printed in Canada.

IT ALL BEGAN ON A TERRIBLE EVENING IN JANUARY, SOMEWHERE IN THE FOOTHILLS OF THE SIERRA SAN JUST.

SOMEWHERE IN THE RUGGED LANDS OF ARAGON, IN THE BITTER COLD OF SPANISH WINTER ON THE HIGH PLATEAUS.

ON THE CRISP SNOW THAT SHROUDED THE THINNING FIELDS OF BARLEY AND WHEAT AS FAR AS THE EYE COULD SEE.

YES, IT ALL BEGAN WHEN TWO CARS AND A TRUCK PULLED UP AT A VILLAGE WHOSE NAME HAD BEEN FORGOTTEN BY EVERYONE. THAT IS, ALMOST EVERYONE...

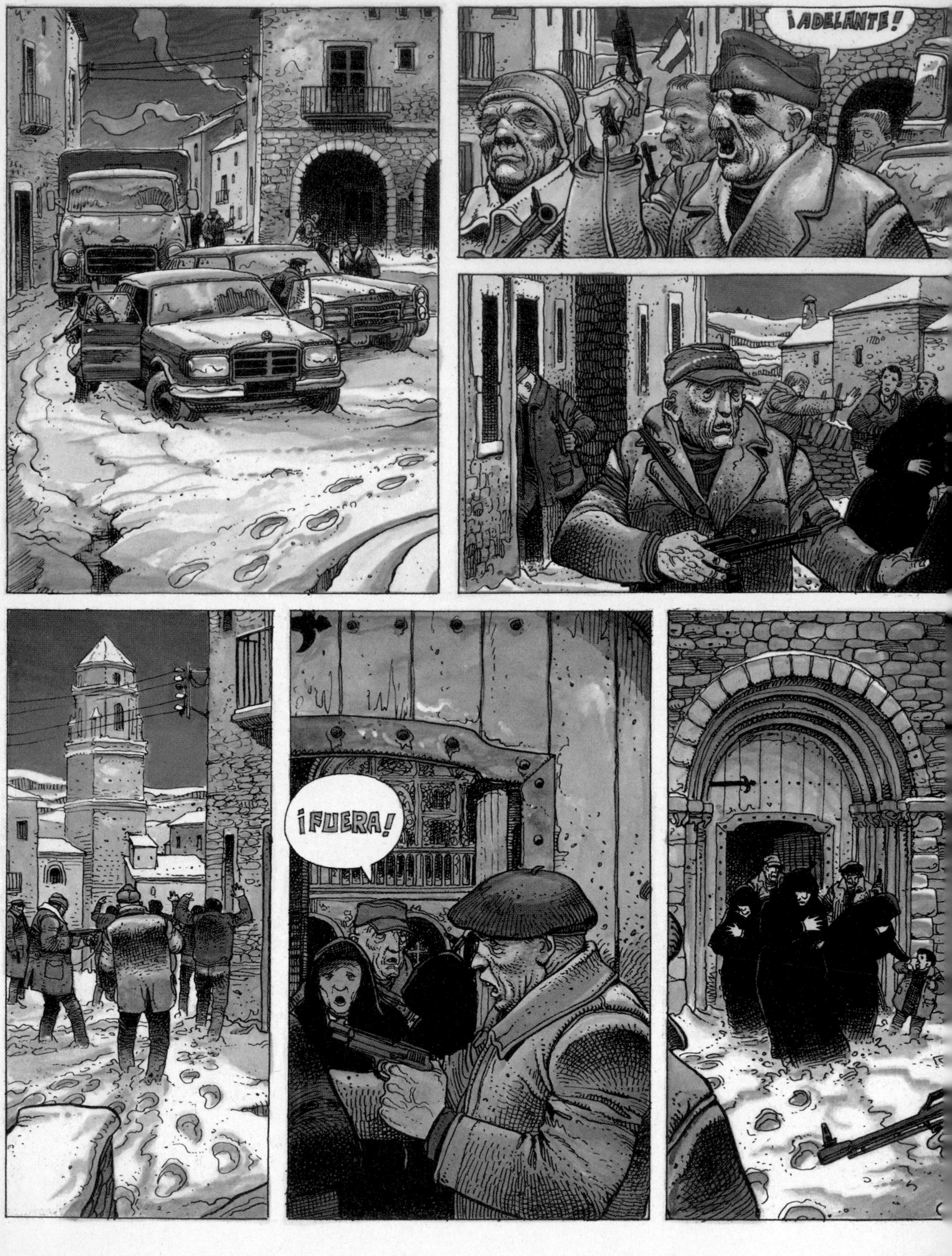
¡ADELANTE!
¡FUERA!

¡HAN REGRESADO!

YOU'RE RIGHT, OLD WOMAN, WE HAVE COME *BACK!* BUT THIS TIME...

PANG

I WON'T MISS.

OUTSIDE, YOU *COMMIE!*

ALL CLEANED UP?

IT WAS TOO EASY.

5

¡AHORA BIEN! ENTONCES QUEMENLO TODO BUENO.

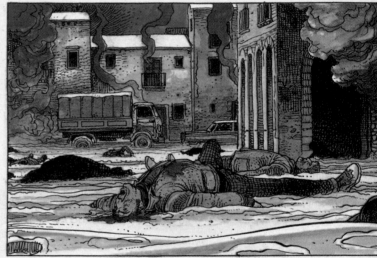

IT WASN'T UNTIL TWO DAYS LATER THAT THE NEWS MADE IT TO FLEET STREET. A GRAY DAY, WITH THE WIND BLOWING HARD OVER LONDON.

HEY, PRITCHARD!

YEAH?

TWO DISPATCHES JUST IN FROM REUTERS.

I THOUGHT YOU'D BE INTERESTED.

HMPH.

SOMETHING TO DO WITH THE SPANISH CIVIL WAR. SINCE YOU'RE ALWAYS TELLING ME ABOUT IT, I THOUGHT...

LET ME SEE.

GT 027 REUTER 16:42
MADRID JANUARY 12
   TERRORISM. ARAGON VILLAGE WIPED OFF THE MAP.

   THE TINY VILLAGE OF NIEVES (POP. 72) WAS COMPLETELY DESTROYED AND ITS ENTIRE POPULATION MASSACRED ON JANUARY 11 AROUND 19.00 (LOCAL TIME). A TERRORIST UNIT BURST INTO THE VILLAGE AND COMMENCED A SYSTEMATIC RAID UPON THE INHABITANTS, INCLUDING WOMEN AND CHILDREN, WHO WERE SLAUGHTERED WITH MACHINE PISTOLS AND HANDGUNS.
   NEXT, THE INVADERS SET FIRE TO THE VILLAGE, WHICH WAS COMPLETELY DESTROYED. THE NEWS WAS DISCOVERED ON JANUARY 12 ONLY BECAUSE OF THE ISOLATION OF THE VILLAGE. THE FIRST RESCUE TEAMS APPARENTLY FOUND NO SURVIVORS.

REUTER 16:53
VILLAGE (CONTD)
ORDED STATEMENT WAS SENT TO A MADRID RADIO STATION
ING RESPONSIBILITY FOR THE ATTACK. THE COMPLETE TEXT
OT YET BEEN MADE PUBLIC. HOWEVER, THE TEXT WAS SENT
THE BLACK ORDER BRIGADE." IT INVOKES "GOOD CHRISTIAN
ES" AND REFERS TO THE COMPLETE DESTRUCTION OF NIEVES AS
EXAMPLE." FURTHER PUNITIVE INCIDENTS ARE TO FOLLOW.
ONE IS REMINDED MOREOVER THAT THE VILLAGE WAS ONE OF THE
CONFLICT BETWEEN THE REPUBLICANS AND THE

MMENCED A SYSTEMATIC RAID UPON THE INHABITANTS, INCLUDING
WOMEN AND CHILDREN, WHO WERE SLAUGHTERED WITH MACHINE PISTOLS
AND HANDGUNS.
   NEXT, THE INVADERS SET FIRE TO THE VILLAGE, WHICH WAS
COMPLETELY DESTROYED. THE NEWS WAS DISCOVERED ON JANUARY 12
ONLY BECAUSE OF THE ISOLATION OF THE VILLAGE. THE FIRST RESCUE
TEAMS APPARENTLY FOUND NO SURVIVORS.

GT 028 REUTER 16:53
   ARAGON VILLAGE (CONTD)
   A RECORDED STATEMENT WAS SENT TO A MADRID RADIO STATION
CLAIMING RESPONSIBILITY FOR THE ATTACK. THE COMPLETE TEXT
HAS NOT YET BEEN MADE PUBLIC. HOWEVER, THE TEXT WAS SENT
BY "THE BLACK ORDER BRIGADE." IT INVOKES "GOOD CHRISTIAN
VALUES" AND REFERS TO THE COMPLETE DESTRUCTION OF NIEVES AS
"AN EXAMPLE." FURTHER PUNITIVE INCIDENTS ARE TO FOLLOW.
   ONE IS REMINDED MOREOVER THAT THE VILLAGE WAS ONE OF THE
PRIMARY ZONES OF CONFLICT BETWEEN THE REPUBLICANS AND THE
FRANQUISTAS THROUGHOUT THE WINTER OF 1938, IN THE SPANISH
CIVIL WAR, BEFORE IT WAS TAKEN BY GEN. CAUDILLO'S TROOPS.
   HOWEVER, DURING THE LAST ELECTION HELD IN THIS LONG-TIME
SYMBOLIC VILLAGE, THE VOTE SWUNG WILDLY TO THE LEFT. THE
NEW MAYOR WAS ONE OF THE VICTIMS OF THE ATTACK.

   NOTE TO EDITORIAL STAFF: A SYNTHESIS WILL BE TRANSMITTED
AT APPROX. 18:00 HRS.

5

WELL, PRITCHARD? WHAT DO YOU THINK?

WHAT DO I THINK? WELL...

SIR! OUR SPANISH CORRESPONDENT HAS JUST PHONED FROM ZARAGOZA.

AH, MY GOOD FRIEND, ATADELL. READ IT TO ME, WILL YOU.

ATTACK CLAIMED BY THE BLACK ORDER BRIGADE. AN UNOFFICIAL BUT DEFINITIVE LIST HAS BEEN CIRCULATED. COMPRISES THE NAMES OF THOSE INVOLVED IN ARAGON. HERE THEY ARE:

MIGUEL VALIÑO, LIEUTENANT, KNOWN FOR HIS RUTHLESSNESS DURING THE SUPPRESSION OF ASTURIAN MINERS DURING THE REPUBLIC, AND PROMOTED TO GENERAL UNDER FRANCO.

JESUS, IT CAN'T BE VALIÑO!

HANS HEINKEL, FORMERLY OF THE CONDOR LEGION, SENT INTO BATTLE BY HITLER. DU BUSQUET, FRENCH, LATER REPORTED AT VICHY, IN THE OAS...

JESUS! THEY'RE ALL THERE!!!

JAVIER, FORMERLY OF THE LEGION AZUL, LENT TO GERMANY BY SPAIN DURING WORLD WAR II; COLPIN, FRENCH MERCENARY RECENTLY RETURNED FROM MAURITANIA; KUYPER, A BELGIAN ACCUSED OF REXISM WHO TOOK REFUGE IN MADRID AND AN ITALIAN, A GREEK, AND A SPANIARD, ALL UNIDENTIFIED.

ALL OF THEM, I TELL YOU!

WHAT DO YOU MEAN "ALL?"

ETTORE PISCIOTTA, FORMER TANK COMMANDER SENT BY MUSSOLINI IN SUPPORT OF FRANCO. JOAQUIN DE VALLELLANO, FALLEN ARISTOCRAT, GUERRILLA MEMBER OF "CHRIST THE KING."

MY GOD! PISCIOTTA, VALLELLANO!

TAKE A LOOK AT THESE PHOTOS, KID. I WAS NEVER GOING TO SHOW THEM TO YOU, BUT NOW...THIS ONE IS NIEVES! OR WAS, I SHOULD SAY. MY BUDDIES AND I IN THE 15TH INTERNATIONAL BRIGADE. WE FOUGHT FOR WEEKS AND WEEKS IN THAT TOWN AGAINST THOSE SONS OF BITCHES WHOSE NAMES YOU JUST HEARD.

IT WAS WHEN THE REPUBLIC WAS STARTING TO BREAK UP. THE COLD WAS AWFUL. WE TOOK THE VILLAGE. THEN LOST IT. THEN TOOK IT AGAIN. THEN LOST IT AGAIN. HUNDREDS KILLED ON BOTH SIDES. IT WAS TERRIBLE.

THAT'S *THEM*, HIGH UP ON THE HILL.

AND THAT'S *US*.

WHAT'S WITH THE FUNNY CLOTHES? EVEN FOR A VOLUNTEER BRIGADE...

HMPH. NO MORE UNIFORMS, NO MORE GUNS, NOTHING. WE STOLE SUITS AND WOOLEN JACKETS FROM THE SHOPS IN TERUEL, AND FOUGHT THEM OFF WITH BOTTLES OF NITROGLYCERINE.

AND THEM?

WELL, IN THE END, THEY WON. MEANWHILE WE, ABANDONED BY THE SOVIETS, BY THE FRENCH, BY EVERYONE...HAD TO FIND OUR WAY BACK TO BARCELONA TO BE REPATRIATED.

EXCEPT THAT HISTORY CONTINUED ITS MARCH, AND NOW THOSE OLD BASTARDS SENSE THAT THE TIMES ARE CHANGING. AND SO...

AND SO YOU HAVE ONE *HELL* OF A STORY THERE, PRITCHARD!

YOU SHOULD SEE MR. DUNCAN ABOUT IT.

HAH! THAT LITTLE SNOB WITH HIS OXFORD ACCENT?!

HOWEVER... PERHAPS YOU'RE RIGHT.

TOC TOC TOC

EDITOR MR. DUNCAN

WHAT DO YOU MEAN TWO COLUMNS AND NO PHOTO AT THE BOTTOM OF PAGE 25?! ARE YOU *FUCKING* KIDDING ME!!?

LOOK, PRITCHARD. ALL THIS IS OLD NEWS THAT NOBODY WANTS TO HEAR ABOUT. TERRORIST ATTACKS ON THE CONTINENT HAPPEN EVERY SINGLE DAY. SO ALL I CAN DO IS...

FINE, FINE...DON'T WEAR YOURSELF OUT. I *GET* THE PICTURE.

LOOK, PRITCHARD...

WELL?

HMPH. JUST FETCH ME A DRINK, WILL YOU.

YOU'RE NOT GOING TO DO ANYTHING?

NO. UNLESS...

UNLESS THIS LOUSY RAG MIGHT STILL BE GOOD FOR SOMETHING! INSTEAD OF DAYDREAMING ABOUT THE PAST TILL I'M BORED OUT OF MY SKULL.

I NEED TO GET UP AND DO SOMETHING! AND SINCE NOBODY GIVES A SHIT ABOUT THE BLACK ORDER, I'LL JUST SEE IF THERE ARE ANY OLD RELICS LEFT LIKE ME WITH STILL ENOUGH IDEALS TO START A NEW ADVENTURE.

OUR LAST ADVENTURE, NO DOUBT. BUT BY GOD IT'LL BE ONE WE REMEMBER!!! BRING ME SOME MORE TELEPHONES, KID!

WHICH IS HOW, AT THAT DAMNED NEWSPAPER'S EXPENSE, PHONE CALLS WENT OFF AROUND THE WORLD LIKE A HAIL OF GUNFIRE.

YOU'VE GOT NEW YORK?

YEAH, HERE.

11

THE FIRST ONE ON BOARD WAS DONAHUE, FROM HIS GRIMY OFFICE IN THE BRONX.

HELLO, IT'S PRITCHARD.

PRITCHARD!!! HOLY SHIT, I NEVER WOULD HAVE GUESSED! WHAT'S...?

ALWAYS READY FOR A BIT OF EXCITEMENT, DONAHUE. AND DOUBTLESSLY TIRED OF PLAYING THE BOSS IN THE BUTCHERS UNION.

HANG ON, I'LL EXPLAIN.

I'M LISTENING, PAL...

SLIGHTLY CORRUPT, HIS UNION, BUT POWERFUL AND RICH! DONAHUE PROMISED TO TAP INTO THEIR RESERVES TO FUND OUR EXPEDITION.

OKAY?

OKAY!

AFTERWARDS, IT WAS BARSAC'S TURN, FORMERLY A HIGH-RANKING FRENCH OFFICER, NOW A CONVERTED PACIFIST.

GETTING HIM TO AGREE WASN'T EASY. BUT BARSAC WAS A MAN OF LOYALTY. ISOLATED IN HIS COUNTRY HOME, HE HESITATED AT FIRST, THEN ACCEPTED.

I COULDN'T REACH AVIDSEN AT HIS MINISTRY. AN EVENING RECEPTION IN ONE OF THE SALONS OF COPENHAGEN. AVIDSEN, A SOCIAL DEMOCRAT, WITH A GLOBAL OUTLOOK...

...BUT ALSO AN ADVENTURER AND A GAMBLER BENEATH HIS REFINED VENEER. HE WAS ALMOST RELIEVED TO JOIN IN. HE MIGHT HAVE BEEN TIRED WITH PLAYING MINISTER.

NO PROBLEM WITH DI MANNO. ALTHOUGH THE LINE TO NAPLES WAS BAD, HE UNDERSTOOD IMMEDIATELY.

AT FIRST, IN TEL-AVIV, THEY PRETENDED THEY HADN'T HEARD OF KATZ. CRAFTY ONES, IN THE ISRAELI SECRET SERVICE...HEH, HEH...

BUT KATZ IS A CURIOUS MAN BY NATURE, AND HE WASN'T HARD TO CONVINCE.

HE FAILED IN HIS CAREER AS A JUDGE, DI MANNO. "OO INDEPENDENT, ALWAYS GETTING INTO TROUBLE WITH BOTH THE LEFT AND THE RIGHT. BUT HE BELIEVED IN DOING THE RIGHT THING.

AND NEITHER WAS STRANSKY, FORMER COMMUNIST, FORMER ENGINEER, FORMER CZECH CITIZEN. HE'S BEEN IN EXILE IN SWITZERLAND SINCE THE PRAGUE SPRING."

AND NEITHER WAS MARIA WIZNIEWSKA, WHO HAD BECOME AN AUTHOR OF CHILDREN'S BOOKS IN WARSAW, BUT WHO HAD NEVER FORGOTTEN HER NIGHTS IN BARCELONA.

AND NEITHER WAS KESSLER. THE GOOD PROFESSOR ALWAYS FOUND UNIVERSITY LIFE ANNOYING, EVEN IN HEIDELBERG. ESPECIALLY SINCE HE'D BEEN UNDER THE THREAT OF OFFICIAL SANCTION ON THE CHARGE OF "INCITING ANARCHY."

THE ONLY ONE TO SAY NO WAS THAT BASTARD RATCLIFF. HE HAD BECOME A SUCCESSFUL HOLLYWOOD SCREENWRITER. HOPE HE ROTS IN HIS SUN DRENCHED BEVERLY HILLS MANSION.

AS FOR O'ROURKE, IT WAS HIS DAUGHTER WHO ANSWERED, TO SAY THAT HE WAS DYING. A STRAY SHOT DURING A RIOT ONE EVENING IN BELFAST. HE WHO HAD ESCAPED SO MANY BULLETS HEADED FOR HIS GENEROUS GUT.

THAT LEFT ONLY CASTEJON. A STRANGE PRIEST, CASTEJON. BUT HE KNEW THE BASQUE COUNTRY LIKE THE BACK OF HIS HAND.

WATCH OUT! THE FRONTIERS ARE VERY WELL PATROLLED THESE DAYS! AND ALTHOUGH SOME OLD MEMBERS OF OUR BRIGADE HAVE LONG BEEN FORGOTTEN, THAT ISN'T THE CASE FOR ALL OF US.

WHICH MEANS...?

HE WAS THE ONE TO SET UP THE PLANS FOR OUR WAY INTO SPAIN. IF CASTEJON HADN'T ENTERED THE LORD'S SERVICE, HE WOULD HAVE ENDED UP A HIRED KILLER OR A GENERAL IN SOME ARMY.

WHICH MEANS YOU'LL RENDEZVOUS IN FRANCE, WHERE I'LL HAVE A FRIEND MEET YOU. WE'LL MEET SOMEWHERE ON THE PAMPLONA ROAD, IN THE MOUNTAINS.

IT TOOK ONE LAST CALL TO EXPLAIN EVERYTHING TO ATADELL, ALSO AN OLD MEMBER OF OUR BRIGADE IN NIEVES. NOW EVERYTHING WAS READY TO GO.

IT WAS A STRANGE FEELING. AND IT WAS GOING TO BE A STRANGE PHONE BILL FOR THE PAPER. BUT THE DIE HAD BEEN CAST...WELL AND TRULY CAST.

IT WAS IN A MOUNTAIN VILLAGE, BEHIND ST. JEAN DE LUZ, THAT THE BIG REUNION TOOK PLACE A COUPLE OF DAYS LATER.

FORTY YEARS AFTER OUR BRIGADE WAS DISBANDED IN 1938!

STRANSKY!!! YOU DIRTY OLD STALINIST!!!

KATZ!!! YOU OLD ZIONIST SCOUNDREL!!!

FORTY YEARS IN WHICH MOST OF US REUNITING IN THE DISCREET BACK ROOM HAD NOT SEEN EACH OTHER.

DARLING MARIA! YOU ARE TRULY RAVISHING!

DEAR BARSAC! STILL SUCH A GENTLEMAN.

IN THIS CASE, FORTY YEARS WAS A LONG TIME.

HOW'S MY OLD FRIEND THE MINISTER?

AND HOW'S MY OLD FRIEND THE PROFESSOR?

ND WHAT'S MORE, WAS A STRANGE OLLECTION OF ASTHMATICS, HEUMATICS AND RTHRITICS, OUR OLD FLESH SWOLLEN BY CHOLESTEROL.

LOOKS LIKE THE UNION GIVES YOU PLENTY TO EAT!

AND YOU, IS LA MAMMA STILL LOOKING AFTER YOU?

BUT STILL, WE WEREN'T A BUNCH OF OLD SENILES YET. IN THE END, IT WAS A GOOD PARTY. IT ALMOST MADE US THINK THAT WE WERE YOUNG AGAIN.

HEY, THERE'S PRITCHARD!

HELLO EVERYONE!

A TOAST!!

WHAT SHOULD WE DRINK TO?

FIRST, TO OUR PAST.

THEN, TO OUR FUTURE!

HA HA... THOSE OLD BLACK ORDER BASTARDS ARE GOING TO RUE THE DAY!

IT'S BEEN A LONG TIME SINCE I'VE FELT LIKE I WAS *REALLY* ALIVE.

MMM...ME, I COULDN'T STOMACH THE IDEA OF DYING WHILE RE-READING KIERKEGAARD WITH MY SLIPPERS ON.

PRITCHARD?

YES?

I'M CASTEJON'S FRENCH CONTACT. I'M THE ONE WHO'S GOING TO TAKE YOU ACROSS THE BORDER.

AHA! AND HOW DO THINGS LOOK?

NOT SO GOOD! THERE'S BEEN UNREST IN THE BASQUE COUNTRY AND THE POLICE ARE BEING RUN RAGGED. THEN THERE'S THE SNOW THAT'S BEEN FALLING FOR THE PAST FEW DAYS.

HMM...

NOT THE BEST, IN OTHER WORDS.

I SUGGEST WE GET MOVING AS SOON AS POSSIBLE.

FINE. NO USE HANGING AROUND, SO...

WHOA, WAIT A MINUTE, FRIENDS! AN INTERNATIONAL BRIGADE REFORMING AFTER FORTY YEARS, THAT'S SOMETHING TO RECORD FOR *POSTERITY!*

ALTHOUGH OUR SPANISH FRIENDS AREN'T HERE.

WE'LL TAKE ANOTHER ONE TOMORROW. IF EVERYTHING GOES WELL.

HOLD STILL NOW.

16

OKAY, IS EVERYBODY READY?

READY!

LET GO, MARIA, I'LL TAKE THAT ONE.

AND I'LL TAKE THIS ONE.

WE START BY BUS!

HERE'S WHERE THE ROAD ENDS. LOAD YOURSELVES UP WHILE I STASH THE BUS.

OKAY!

ATCHOO!

GRR...DAMN SHOELACES!

DAMN! I'VE BEEN WORKING IN WARM COUNTRIES FOR TOO LONG! MY OLD COAT DOESN'T FIT ANYMORE!

IT WILL TAKE A GOOD HOUR'S CLIMB TO REACH THE BORDER.

15

ACROSS THE BORDER THERE'S A TAVERN WHERE WE CAN STOP IF ALL IS CLEAR.

HUFF...

YOU OKAY, MARIA?

MY FEET ARE FREEZING.

ATCHOO!

GODDAMN! I'M THINKING WE'RE TOO OLD FOR A CLIMB LIKE THIS!

THERE'S THE BORDER.

AND DOWN THERE, THE TAVERN.

ATCHOO!

THE LIGHT MEANS IT'S ALL CLEAR. AN OLD SMUGGLER'S SIGNAL. WE CAN HEAD DOWN.

I FEEL LIKE SHIT!

STRONG, SWEET COFFEE FOR EVERYONE!

JUST HAND ME A BOTTLE OF WHISKEY INSTEAD!

LISTEN, THAT MIGHT NOT BE SUCH A GOOD IDEA IF...

AH, DON'T WORRY ABOUT IT, MY FRIEND. BESIDES, I'M NOT GOING TO BE AROUND MUCH LONGER ANYWAY.

DON'T TALK LIKE THAT, DONAHUE!

AH...AHH... ATCHOO!

WE SHOULD GO. IT'S PAST MIDNIGHT.

LET'S GO.

UP AGAIN?

NOT FOR LONG. BUT ON THE OTHER SIDE IS WHERE THINGS COULD GO WRONG. BECAUSE JUST BEHIND THAT RIDGE IS WHERE...

HELP ME, KESSLER, I'M SLIPPING!

AAHH!

WHAT'S HAPPENING?

GOOD GOD! THAT WAS DONAHUE!!!

SHIT! I HOPE HE'S NOT...

19

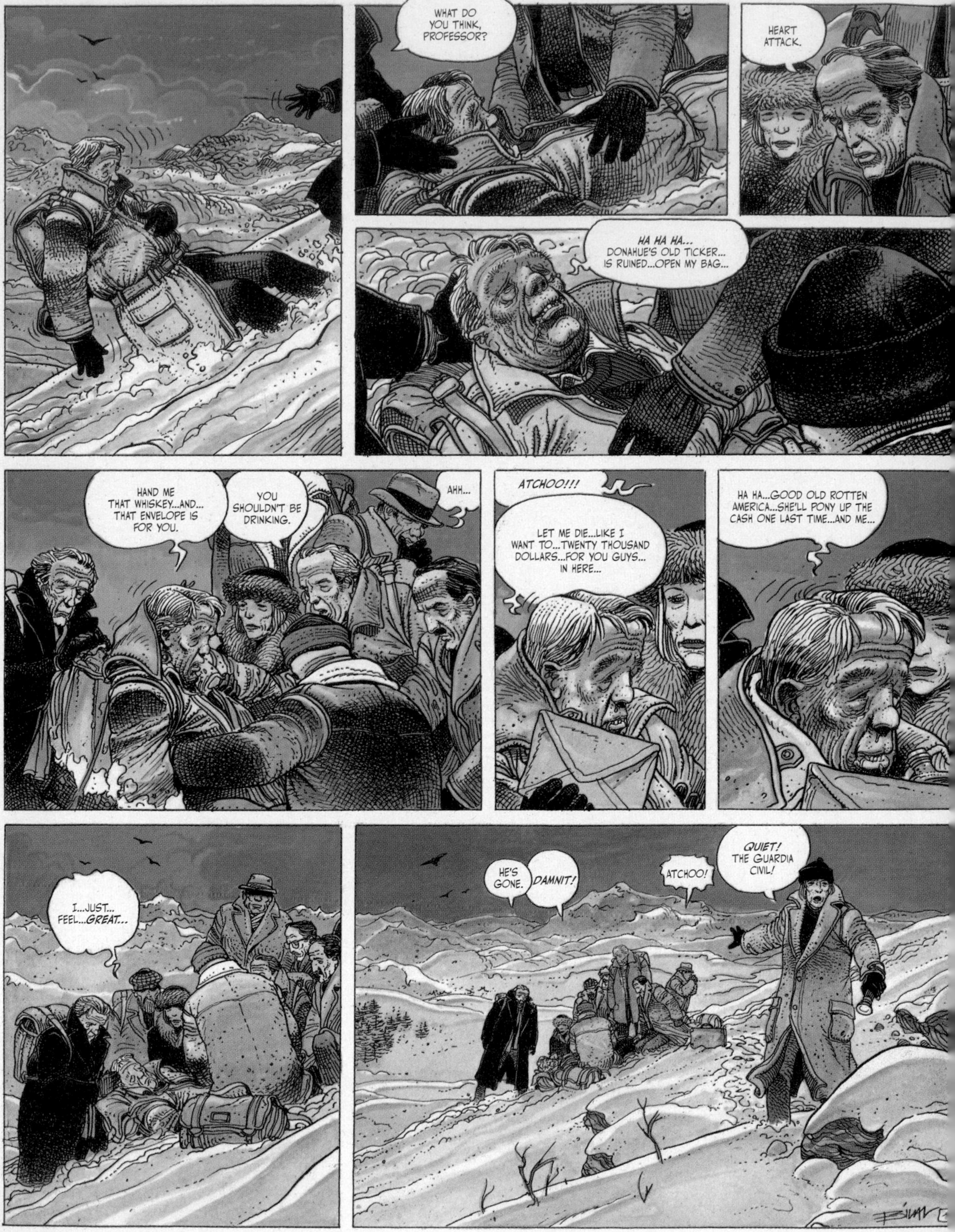
WHAT DO YOU THINK, PROFESSOR?
HEART ATTACK.
HA HA HA... DONAHUE'S OLD TICKER... IS RUINED...OPEN MY BAG...
HAND ME THAT WHISKEY...AND... THAT ENVELOPE IS FOR YOU.
YOU SHOULDN'T BE DRINKING.
AHH...
ATCHOO!!!
LET ME DIE...LIKE I WANT TO...TWENTY THOUSAND DOLLARS...FOR YOU GUYS... IN HERE...
HA HA...GOOD OLD ROTTEN AMERICA...SHE'LL PONY UP THE CASH ONE LAST TIME...AND ME...
I...JUST... FEEL...GREAT...
HE'S GONE.
DAMNIT!
ATCHOO!
QUIET! THE GUARDIA CIVIL!

WE HAVE TO RUN!

BUT DONAHUE? WE CAN'T JUST LEAVE HIM HERE!

JUST AFTER THE LARGE OAK FOREST, YOU'LL SEE AN ABANDONED FARMHOUSE. WAIT THERE! IN DUE TIME, CASTEJON WILL COME AND GET YOU. BUT REMEMBER... NO LIGHTS!

THANK YOU, MY FRIEND!

I'LL TAKE CARE OF IT! THE MAIN THING IS THAT THEY DON'T SEE YOU. WHILE I CREATE A DIVERSION TRYING TO GET BACK TO FRANCE, YOU'LL ALL HEAD DOWN ALONG THIS VALLEY.

THAT'S IT! THEY'VE SPOTTED US! IF I CAN JUST REACH THAT RAVINE.

¡POR AQUI!

BRATATAC

AAAH!

WE DESCENDED THROUGH THE IMMENSE OAK FOREST IN ABSOLUTE SILENCE. THE ONLY SOUND WAS THE SNOW CRUNCHING UNDER OUR WEARY FEET.

WE HAD ALL HEARD THE GUNSHOTS, AND THE AVALANCHE, BUT NONE OF US SAID A WORD.

CASTEJON ARRIVED AT THE FARMHOUSE JUST BEFORE DAWN. AT FIRST GLANCE, HE ALREADY KNEW THAT ONE OF US WAS MISSING.

ATCHOO!

YOU'LL RIDE IN THERE TILL WE GET TO THE CHURCH! LET'S GO, COMPAÑEROS! THIS AREA IS HEAVILY GUARDED, BUT WE'LL GET THROUGH.

INDEED, WE GOT THROUGH. CASTEJON HAD CHARTERED A RUN-DOWN OLD BUS UNDER THE PRETENSE OF ARRANGING A PILGRIMAGE TO CATALONIA.

RATTLING ALONG THE DESERTED ROADS TOWARDS ZARAGOZA, AMONG BLACK-CLAD WOMEN EATING CHORIZO, WE ALL SAT THINKING, PERHAPS ABOUT DONAHUE.

AND PERHAPS ABOUT DEATH ITSELF, AS PEOPLE DO WHEN THEY AGE, KNOWING IT WAITS FOR THEM, INSIDIOUS, YET AT THE SAME TIME FAMILIAR.

ATCHOOO!

AND PERHAPS SOME OF THE OTHERS WERE ALSO THINKING ABOUT ATADELL, AND THE RENDEZVOUS THAT HAD BEEN PLANNED IN THE SUBURBS OF BARCELONA.

EXCEPT THAT THE RENDEZVOUS WAS NEVER TO TAKE PLACE... BECAUSE AFTER WE HAD DROPPED OFF CASTEJON'S FLOCK AT THE SAGRADA FAMILIA...

21

23

AFTER WE HAD TRAVERSED THE CITY'S LONG AVENUES, WHICH BROUGHT BACK SO MANY MEMORIES FOR THOSE WHO HAD PATROLLED THEM IN ARMS ALL THOSE YEARS AGO.

IS THIS IT?

WHAT'S HAPPENING?

DON'T KNOW.

HOW MUCH?

85 PESETAS, SEÑOR.

DIDN'T YOU HEAR IT ON THE RADIO?

THERE WAS A *MASSIVE* EXPLOSION!

SEEMS THE PLACE WAS FILLED WITH OLD CRACKPOTS. ANARCHISTS, FROM THE OLD CONFEDERACIÓN NACIONAL DEL TRABAJO.

AND TROTSKYISTS, FROM THE POUM.

ALL THESE *BULLSHIT* UNDERGROUND ACTIVITIES FROM THE OLD DAYS, I DON'T SEE WHAT THEY'RE GOOD FOR.

THEY'RE GOOD FOR KNOCKING BACK DEMOCRATIC PROGRESS, THAT'S WHAT.

AND WHAT ABOUT THAT BLACK ORDER BRIGADE THAT CLAIMED THE ATTACK? THERE'S ANOTHER INTERESTING BUNCH.

JUST ANOTHER TYPE OF BASTARD!

THEY'RE CERTAINLY NO BETTER.

A LOT WORSE, YOU MEAN

IT'S ALL JUST OLD NEWS!

DAMNIT! ALREADY TWO OF US ARE DEAD. AND WE DON'T KNOW A DAMN THING ABOUT WHAT'S REALLY GOING ON.

ATADELL HAD PHONED TO TELL ME HE WAS HOPING TO GET SOME INFORMATION THERE, BECAUSE HE'D HEARD THE BLACK ORDER WAS PLANNING SOMETHING IN BARCELONA.

LET'S GET OUT OF HERE!

DID YOU HEAR WHAT THEY WERE SAYING?

YES AND I FOUND IT ALL VERY UPSETTING. FOR US AS WELL AS THE OTHERS, I MEAN...

POOR ATADELL. LOOKS LIKE HE GOT HIS INFORMATION AFTER ALL.

TOO MUCH OF IT, OR NOT ENOUGH! THE INFORMATION GAME ISN'T FORGIVING OF THOSE KINDS OF MISTAKES, TAKE IT FROM A SPECIALIST.

AH, THOSE BASTARDS!

YES... THEY'RE POWERFUL...

SEÑOR...

?

NOT TO MENTION THAT NOW WE'RE COMPLETELY CUT OFF.

AND COMPLETELY EXHAUSTED.

ATCHOOO!

WHAT...?!

23

WHAT DOES IT SAY?

WELL, WHAT DO WE DO?

FIRST, A HOTEL, SO I CAN TAKE OFF THIS DAMN ROBE.

TRUE. DRESSED LIKE THIS WE MUST ALL LOOK LIKE...

OLD TERRORISTS FROM A FORGOTTEN AGE, PROBABLY.

ATCHOOO!!

THE HOSTAL DE LOS REYES, THEN... IF IT'S STILL THERE. AT LEAST THAT WILL BRING BACK A FEW GOOD MEMORIES.

YOU'RE RIGHT, MARIA. WE NEED A PLACE TO REST AND GET OUR STRENGTH BACK.

THAT'S RIGHT, GOOD IDEA.

ME, I'VE GOT A COLD FROM ALL THIS STRENUOUS EXERCISE.

BE AT LAS RAMBLAS THIS AFTERNOON. VISIT THE PARROT-SELLER AND ASK HIM IF HE HAS A TALKATIVE BIRD.

HMM... THIS PLACE HAS AGED A BIT.

YEAH, LOOKS LIKE WE'RE NOT THE ONLY ONES.

ACTUALLY IT MAKES ME FEEL YOUNGER.

SO, WE'LL MEET IN AN HOUR?

FINE. I CAN'T WAIT TO SEE LAS RAMBLAS AGAIN.

I'M READY!

WELL, LET'S GO PLAY EXOTIC BIRD LOVERS THEN.

SHOULD WE CALL A DOCTOR?

DON'T EVEN THINK ABOUT IT! COLDS CLEAR UP JUST FINE ON THEIR OWN.

YOU'RE NOT SORRY YOU LEFT WARSAW TO COME JOIN US, MARIA?

NOT YET, PRITCH, NOT YET...

THERE, LOOK! PARROTS!

THAT MUST BE HIM. LET'S SEE.

AHEM...WE'RE LOOKING FOR A TALKATIVE BIRD.

CERTAINLY, I HAVE AN EXCELLENT ONE HERE.

WHAT CAN IT SAY?

IT SAYS, FOR EXAMPLE, THAT YOUR FRIEND ATADELL KEPT *BAD* COMPANY, AND MADE THE MISTAKE OF TRYING TO GET INFORMATION ON THE BLACK ORDER THROUGH THE HIGHER-UPS IN THE MINISTRY OF THE INTERIOR. PEOPLE WHO PRETENDED THEY HAD FORGOTTEN CERTAIN THINGS STARTED TAKING AN INTEREST IN HIM. THE BLACK ORDER HAS MANY FRIENDS IN THE POLICE FORCE. IN *EVERY* POLICE FORCE...

AND WHAT ELSE?

IT SAYS THAT WE TOO HAVE OUR INFORMANTS. THE MEN OF THE BLACK ORDER HAVE PULLED OFF TWO SUCCESSFUL ATTACKS IN OUR COUNTRY, BUT THEY HAVE INTERNATIONAL AMBITIONS, AND AREN'T PLANNING TO STAY AROUND HERE VERY LONG, FOR A NUMBER OF REASONS.

THEY'RE SUPPOSED TO LEAVE FOR SICILY LATE TONIGHT. A GREEK SHIP-OWNER SYMPATHETIC TO THEIR PLANS HAS PUT HIS YACHT, NEMESIS, AT THEIR DISPOSAL. THAT'S ALL MY BIRD KNOWS.

TRULY A TALENTED CREATURE.

YES, WELL DONE, POLLY!

I CAN TELL YOU'RE ANXIOUS TO GET BACK TO THE HOTEL AND PLAN OUR STRATEGY, RIGHT PRITCH?

LET'S SAY I'M FEELING A LITTLE MORE HOPEFUL. BUT FIRST...

THIS BOUQUET FOR THE LADY.

MUY BIEN, SEÑOR.

27

THE DECISION WAS QUICKLY MADE, DESPITE SOME RESERVATIONS. BUT A VOTE WAS REQUIRED.

MY FRIENDS, DO YOU REALLY BELIEVE WE SHOULD STOOP TO THE METHODS OF THESE CRIMINALS?

DON'T BE AN ASS, BARSAC. I'M THE PRIEST HERE, AND I'LL TAKE CARE OF OUR SOULS.

PUT IT TO A VOTE THEN?

GOOD IDEA!

IN THE END, WE ALL RECOGNIZED THAT WE HAD TO AVENGE THE DEAD AND DELIVER A WARNING TO THE BLACK ORDER.

ALRIGHT THEN, CASTEJON WILL TAKE CARE OF FINDING THE NECESSARY EQUIPMENT.

I HAVE AN EXCELLENT CONTACT FOR THIS SORT OF THING.

WE ALSO HAD TO WATCH THE HARBOR, WHILE MAKING PLANS FOR OUR OWN DEPARTURE.

I'LL KEEP AN EYE ON THE YACHT.

AND I'LL GO EXPLORE THE DOCKS. WITH SOME "GREASING OF THE WHEELS" I MIGHT FIND MYSELF SOME NEW BEST FRIENDS.

THEY'LL COME IN HANDY, BECAUSE IF WE MAKE THE TYPE OF ATTACK YOU'RE TALKING ABOUT, THERE'LL BE NO WAY WE CAN HANG AROUND HERE FOR LONG.

HEY KATZ, DON'T FORGET DONAHUE'S CASH!

IN CASE WE HAVE TO MAKE A SUDDEN DEPARTURE, I'M GOING TO GET SOME THINGS AT THE PHARMACY FOR DI MANNO. WILL YOU COME WITH ME, MARIA?

ACTUALLY, KESSLER, I'D RATHER GET SOME SLEEP. IT'S SHAPING UP TO BE ANOTHER LONG NIGHT.

ON A WARM NIGHT IN THE GRAND CITY, WE MADE OUR WAY DOWN TO THE HARBOR AS DISCREETLY AS WE COULD.

RENFE METRO

THINK WE'LL DO IT, JUDGE?

IT'LL GO FINE, STRANSKY. DON'T YOU WORRY.

OKAY, WE'LL ALL MEET AT THE HARBOR IN THREE HOURS AT THE LATEST.

OKAY!

ATCHOOO!

THROUGH THE NARROW STREETS OF THE "BARRIO CHINO," NOTHING WAS EASIER THAN INTERMINGLING WITH THE TIGHTLY PACKED CROWD AS THEY STROLLED PAST ALL THE RESTAURANTS WITH THEIR ENTICING ODORS.

ALL WAS QUIET ON THE HARBOR.

WELL?

THERE'S THE NEMESIS. IF YOU ASK ME, THEY'RE NEARLY ALL ABOARD.

BUT THAT BOAT AT THE DOCK WITH THOSE TWO GREEK SAILORS MEANS THEY'RE STILL WAITING FOR SOMEONE. THAT'S OUR ONLY POSSIBLE TARGET.

EXCELLENT! I HAVE JUST THE THING FOR OUR LATECOMERS.

MY GOD, IT'S AN ANTIQUITY FROM BEFORE THE WAR!

YES, IT'LL BRING BACK MEMORIES FOR THOSE BASTARDS!

ANYWAY, WE'LL HAVE TO ACT QUICKLY.

I'M STILL A GOOD SWIMMER. LET ME DO IT.

LOOK, RSAC, IF YOU 'N'T APPROVE, U DON'T HAVE TO DO IT.

IT DOESN'T MATTER, MARIA. AFTER ALL, WE REACHED OUR DECISION DEMOCRATICALLY.

I KNEW YOU HADN'T CHANGED.

IZNALLOZ
BARCELONA

29

WATCH OUT, SOMEONE'S COMING!

HIJO DE PUTA! THE ONE ON THE LEFT IS THAT OLD BASTARD FROM OPUS DEI WHO I MET SO LONG AGO!

AND THE OTHER ONE LOOKS LIKE KUYPER, THE BELGIAN. HE'S ANOTHER OLD SON-OF-A-BITCH.

HIC!

ATCHOO!

LORD! WHAT'S BARSAC DOING?

SHHHH... NOT NOW...

BAH...THEY'RE DRUNK AND ROARING OUT THAT FRANCO'S OLD ANTHEM, THERE'S NO WAY THEY'LL HEAR US.

¡VAMOS! EURP... CARA AL... SOL

♫HIPS...♫ CARA... AL ... SOL

HIC

BRAOUM

WELL DONE, FRIENDS! GREAT FIREWORKS!

OH, SO THERE YOU ARE!

HERE, BARSAC. COVER UP!

HURRY! WE'RE GOING TO HAVE TO GET OUT OF HERE.

DID YOU SEE THAT? THE YACHT JUST RAISED ANCHOR.

YEAH, AND WE'LL BE RAISING ANCHOR SOON, TOO.

YOU FOUND SOMETHING?

AN EGYPTIAN CARGO SHIP LEAVING FOR PALERMO AT DAWN. I'LL HAVE TO ASK YOU NOT TO LET THEM KNOW THAT I'M A JEW, A ZIONIST, AND A SPY IN THE BARGAIN.

THEY THINK I'M A RELATIVELY HONEST LIBYAN MERCHANT EVADING A TRIAL WITH SOME BUSINESS PARTNERS.

CARMES

ANYWAY, WITH ALL THE CASH THEY'LL GET FROM US, THEY WON'T BE TOO CURIOUS.

HOW MUCH?

A THOUSAND DOLLARS A HEAD. BUT THE POLICE WON'T FIND US IN THE COMPARTMENT THEY'RE SETTING UP FOR US.

RATHER UNCOMFORTABLE, THEN...?

YES, BUT THEN...

AND WHAT TIME DO WE LEAVE?

SIX IN THE MORNING. THEY DON'T WANT US ABOARD THEIR RUSTY IRON HEAP BEFORE THEN.

FINE. FROM HERE ON WE SPLIT UP FOR A WHILE, AND PLAY GOOD INNOCENT TOURISTS.

29

NOT MUCH WAS LEFT OF THE NIGHT, YET NONETHELESS IT SEEMED A LONG ONE.

IT'S BEEN A LONG TIME SINCE I'VE SEEN MEN DIE, AVIDSEN.

YES, IT'S AN UGLY THING. BUT YOU KNOW, IN MY COUNTRY, AS WELL-POLICED AS IT IS, I'VE SEEN MANY OTHER THINGS, JUST AS UGLY.

THE BITTERSWEET "HIERBA" ALCOHOL IN THE BACK ROOM OF A FRIENDLY BAR DIDN'T REALLY LIFT OUR SPIRITS.

WE USED DIRTY METHODS, WHICH DIDN'T GIVE US ANY HONOR.

YOU'RE RIGHT, JUDGE. AND THOSE GREEK SAILORS SHOULDN'T HAVE BEEN INVOLVED AT ALL.

YOU'RE NOT GOING TO GIVE US A CRISIS OF FAITH, ARE YOU, BARSAC?

AND THE SAVORY AND SECRET "TAPAS" OF A BAR WITH UNINQUISITIVE CUSTOMERS DIDN'T REALLY SOOTHE OUR STOMACHS.

COME NOW, YOU KNOW VERY WELL THAT REVOLUTIONARY VIOLENCE ONLY REACTS TO THE VIOLENCE OF THE ESTABLISHED ORDER.

BUT I ALSO KNOW THAT LEFTIST TERRORISM HAS NEVER RESOLVED ANYTHING. IN THE END I'M WONDERING IF I SHOULDN'T HAVE GOTTEN YOU ALL INVOLVED IN THIS OLD FOLKS' CRUSADE.

IN THE EARLY MORNING, WHEN WE HAD TO MEET THE AKHIM, WE WERE ALL SILENT AFTER COLLECTING OUR BAGS. VERY SILENT...

WHICH WAS BETTER. MUCH BETTER...

THE CARGO SHIP WAS FILTHY, AND THE COMPARTMENT THAT HAD BEEN SET UP IN THE HOLD REEKED OF VOMIT, URINE, ORANGE PEELS AND CLOVES.

IT WAS IN THOSE CRAMPED QUARTERS THAT WE HAD TO SPEND THE MONOTONOUS DAYS OF THE DYING OLD TUB'S LONG VOYAGE.

COUGH, COUGH, COUGH....

BADLY PLAYED CARD GAMES AND REVOLTING MEALS FOLLOWED ONE AFTER ANOTHER IN THE FOUL COMPARTMENT. DI MANNO WAS AS SICK AS A DOG.

ONE EVENING, DOLPHINS FOLLOWED THE BOAT, PLAYING AROUND IT LIKE WELL-BEHAVED CHILDREN, BRINGING US HOPE AND JOY.

IT WAS ONLY IN SIGHT OF PALERMO THAT HE BEGAN TO GET BETTER, WHICH WAS JUST IN TIME.

AKHIM

BECAUSE, AS SOON AS WE WERE SETTLED IN A RUN-DOWN HARBORSIDE HOVEL, WHICH ENABLED US TO AVOID CUTTING TOO DEEPLY INTO THE CASH BEQUEATHED BY DONAHUE, WE HAD TO GET SOME INFORMATION.

LA STA

AND THAT WAS UP TO HIM.

I WAS TOLD THAT THE NEMESIS PUT INTO PORT HERE SIX DAYS AGO. ABOUT TEN GUYS GOT OFF...AND PFFFT... THAT'S IT...

HMM...TO FIND OUT WHERE THEY WENT, I CAN THINK OF ONLY ONE MAN...DON CALOGERO VIRZI.

DON CALOGERO?

YES, VERY OLD MAFIOSO.

BUT WILL HE TALK?

I BELIEVE SO. YOU SEE, I STRUGGLED TO HAVE HIM LOCKED UP IN THE FIFTIES. AND HE ATTEMPTED TO HAVE A FEW OF HIS HITMEN KNOCK ME OFF IN THE SIXTIES.

BOTH OF US FAILED. WHICH IS WHY HE'S FREE, AND I'M ALIVE. NOW HE'S AN OLD DON WHO DOES ME THE HONOR OF CONSIDERING ME ONE OF THE *FEW* HONEST JUDGES OF HIS LONG CAREER.

AND SINCE I, MYSELF, HAVE TO ACKNOWLEDGE THAT DESPITE HIS CROOKED DEALINGS HE AT LEAST HAS DIGNITY, I'LL TRY TO FIND HIM AGAIN.

WE'LL START WITH A SMALL-TIME GANGSTER I KNOW OF, SALVATORE ACCURSIO.

I'LL GO WITH YOU.

WHAT DO YOU MEAN YOU DON'T KNOW DON CALOGERO? TELL ME, SALVATORE, DO YOU HAVE ANY IDEA HOW MANY WARRANTS THERE ARE WITH YOUR NAME ON THEM ON MY DESK IN NAPLES?

UM...ACTUALLY I DO HAVE A LEAD FOR YOU, DOTTORE.

DON CALOGERO? HE HASN'T BEEN IN PALERMO FOR A LONG TIME.

I KNOW, HE RETIRED. BUT *WHERE?*

SEND THEM TO LEONARDO INSTEAD, SO THEY'LL LEAVE US ALONE!

JUST A MINUTE, I HAVE TO MAKE A CALL.

OF COURSE, LEONARDO, GO AHEAD.

A GLASS OF WINE?

WON'T SAY "NO."

THE RENTAL CAR ROLLED FOR A LONG TIME ALONG THE RUN-DOWN COUNTRY ROADS.

THE TOWN WAS NAMED REGALPETRA. IN THE OLD DAYS, THE SALT MINE HAD MADE ITS FORTUNE.

NOW EVERYTHING THERE WAS DEAD...THE PEOPLE AND THE TOWN...

EXCEPT FOR DON CALOGERO'S VILLA, WHERE THE DOGS WERE AS BIG AS THE BODYGUARDS. THE GARDEN BLOOMED INTENSELY, THE AIR WAS CLEAN AND REFRESHING...

PREGO!

PA-T5 2367

MADE IT AT LAST, YOU DAMN JUDGE!

UH, YES. I HAVE SOMETHING TO ASK YOU.

MMM...I KNOW WHAT YOU WANT.

?

YOU DO?

REALLY, NOW. I'M NOT SENILE AND I'VE KEPT SOME OF MY FRIENDS IN PALERMO.

SO WHAT ARE YOU SUGGESTING?

THAT I PROVIDE YOU WITH INFORMATION ABOUT SOME OLD MEN LIKE YOU AND ME. AND IN *EXCHANGE*...

IN EXCHANGE?

IT WAS HARD FOR DI MANNO, THE HONEST JUDGE. REALLY HARD. AFTER ALL, HUSHING UP A DIRTY DRUG RING TRAFFICKING SOMEWHERE IN THE DEPTHS OF ANATOLA...

JUST TO LEARN IN EXCHANGE THAT THE BLACK ORDER WAS IN ROME TO KIDNAP A COMMUNIST LEADER AND MAKE THE I.C.P. COUGH UP A HEFTY RANSOM TO ADD TO THEIR WAR CHEST/COFFERS...

PERHAPS IT WAS WORTH IT...

...OR PERHAPS NOT.

IN ANY CASE, TWO DAYS LATER, AFTER A BRIEF CROSSING OVER A STORMY SEA, IT WAS DECIDED TO TAKE THE TRAIN TO ROME, SO TO BE DISCREET, AND TO STRETCH OUR FUNDS.

YOU DON'T WANT TO STOP AND SAY HI TO "LA MAMMA" IN NAPLES?

HMPH...I DON'T REALLY KNOW IF SHE'D BE VERY PROUD OF ME RIGHT *NOW*.

ONCE INSTALLED IN A HUMBLE SUITE IN THE TRASTEVERE, WE ALL STARTED CHASING CLUES, BECAUSE WE STILL NEEDED TO FIND OUT HOW AND WHERE OUR QUARRY WAS GETTING ABOUT IN THE CITY. AND SINCE WE COULDN'T WORK IN THE OPEN....

HOTEL

STRANSKY HOPED THAT GOOD OLD PROLETARIAN INTERNATIONALISM WOULD WORK FAVOR WITH HIS OLD COMRADES FROM THE COMMUNIST PARTY.

PAESE SERA

MAKING TELEPHONE CALLS LEFT AND RIGHT, KATZ WORKED HIS CONTACTS IN THE SECRET SERVICE, AND...

...VIDSEN WANTED TO SOUND OUT THE LOCAL SOCIALISTS, OR AT LEAST, WHAT WAS LEFT OF THEM, WHICH ONLY PRODUCED A LOT IN RESTAURANT BILLS.

AS FOR MARIA, SHE HAD GOTTEN BACK IN TOUCH WITH FORGOTTEN FRIENDS, AND MUCH PREFERRED ATTENDING PARTIES IN AMBER-COLORED PALACES.

DI MANNO MET WITH UNSAVORY COPS IN FRONT OF ELEGANT BUBBLING FOUNTAINS...

AND ONE MORNING, AS THE DAYS WERE GETTING WARMER, SOMEWHERE IN THE RUINS OF THE ROMAN FORUM...

TO THINK THAT THOSE OLD BASTARD COMRADES ARE PRETENDING THEY DON'T KNOW ME ANYMORE SINCE I LEFT PRAGUE, AND THAT PARTY!

AS FOR ME, ALL I'VE LEARNED IS THAT ITALIAN COUNTER-INTELLIGENCE ISN'T WORTH A DAMN!

THAT DOESN'T SURPRISE ME. ON THE OTHER HAND, THE POLICE KNOW SOMETHING, BUT THE SECRET'S TOO CLOSELY GUARDED FOR USUAL INFORMANTS.

AS FOR THE BOURGEOIS POLITICAL PARTIES, THEY'RE TOO INVOLVED WITH STARTING "COMBINAZIONE" TO WORRY ABOUT THE FUTURE PROBLEMS OF COMMUNISTS, WHICH WOULD BE TO THEIR BENEFIT.

IN SHORT, WE STRUCK OUT EVERYWHERE!

NOT AT ALL, PRITCH, NOT AT ALL!

MARIA! WE GAVE UP WAITING FOR YOU!

WELL, I FOUND OUT THE BLACK ORDER'S HIDING PLACE OVER THE COURSE OF YESTERDAY'S SOIRÉE, BETWEEN THE PISTACHIO SORBET AND THE FRENCH CHAMPAGNE.

HOT DAMN, MARIA!

THEY'RE IN A VERY BEAUTIFUL PALACE IN THE HILLS BEHIND ST. PETER'S.

FRIENDS OF EITHER THE LATE VALERIO BORGHESE, THE BLACK PRINCE, OR THAT CRAZY OLD HAG ELVINA PALLAVICINI!!?

A YOUNG GUATEMALAN PRELATE HERE FOR AN AUDIENCE WITH THE POPE DROPPED THE LOCATION WITHOUT REALIZING IT.

THE YOUNG FOOL WAS DEAD DRUNK AND HAD JUST RETURNED FROM PEEING BEHIND A CLUMP OF CAMELLIAS, WHERE HE HAD OVERHEARD SOMEONE SPEAKING SPANISH.

AH, THE CLERGY THESE DAYS...

FOR CHRIST'S SAKE TELL US!!

36

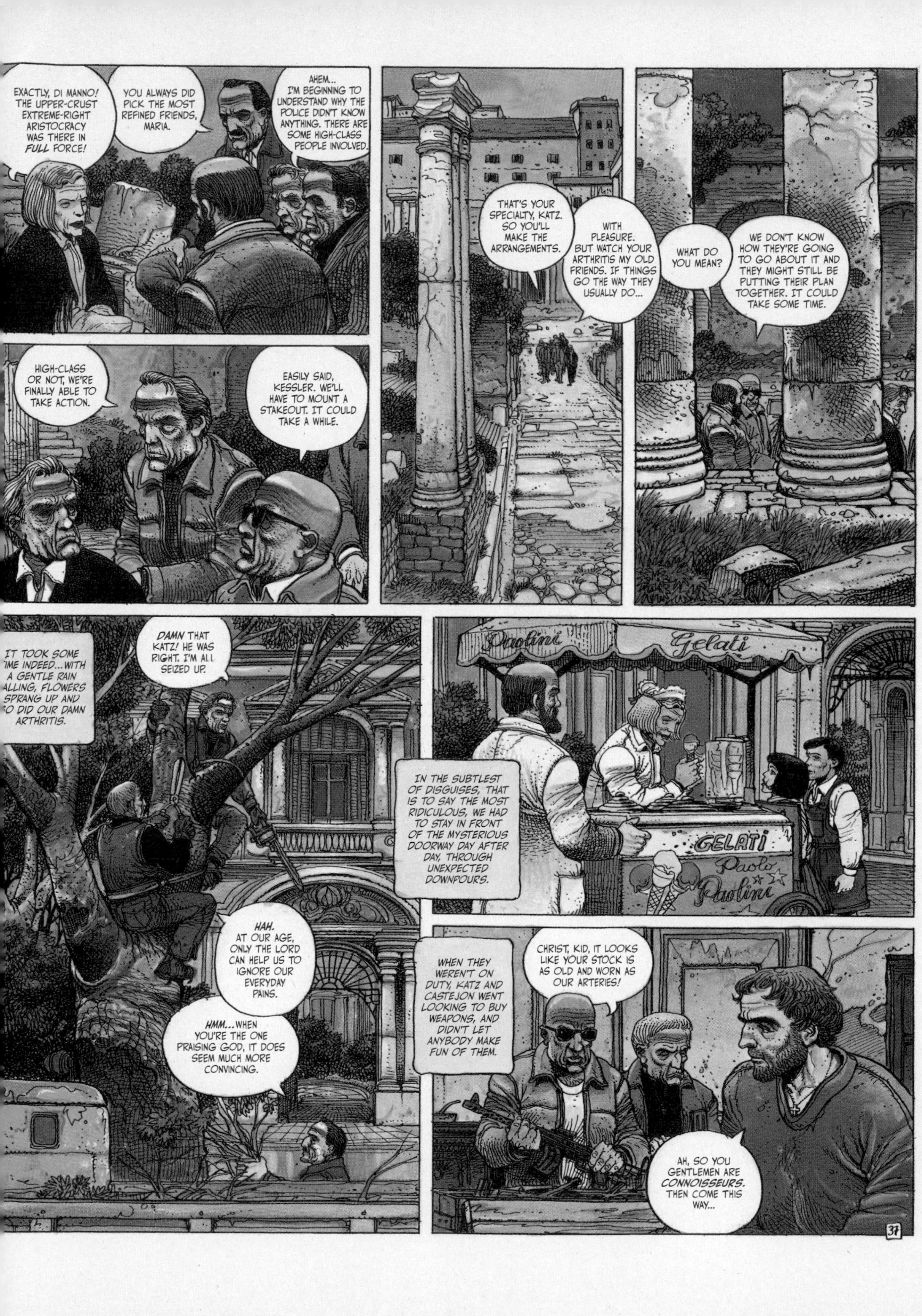
EXACTLY, DI MANNO! THE UPPER-CRUST EXTREME-RIGHT ARISTOCRACY WAS THERE IN FULL FORCE!
YOU ALWAYS DID PICK THE MOST REFINED FRIENDS, MARIA.
AHEM... I'M BEGINNING TO UNDERSTAND WHY THE POLICE DIDN'T KNOW ANYTHING. THERE ARE SOME HIGH-CLASS PEOPLE INVOLVED.
HIGH-CLASS OR NOT, WE'RE FINALLY ABLE TO TAKE ACTION.
EASILY SAID, KESSLER. WE'LL HAVE TO MOUNT A STAKEOUT. IT COULD TAKE A WHILE.
THAT'S YOUR SPECIALTY, KATZ. SO YOU'LL MAKE THE ARRANGEMENTS.
WITH PLEASURE. BUT WATCH YOUR ARTHRITIS MY OLD FRIENDS. IF THINGS GO THE WAY THEY USUALLY DO...
WHAT DO YOU MEAN?
WE DON'T KNOW HOW THEY'RE GOING TO GO ABOUT IT AND THEY MIGHT STILL BE PUTTING THEIR PLAN TOGETHER. IT COULD TAKE SOME TIME.
IT TOOK SOME TIME INDEED...WITH A GENTLE RAIN FALLING, FLOWERS SPRANG UP AND SO DID OUR DAMN ARTHRITIS.
DAMN THAT KATZ! HE WAS RIGHT. I'M ALL SEIZED UP.
HAH. AT OUR AGE, ONLY THE LORD CAN HELP US TO IGNORE OUR EVERYDAY PAINS.
HMM...WHEN YOU'RE THE ONE PRAISING GOD, IT DOES SEEM MUCH MORE CONVINCING.
Paolini Gelati
IN THE SUBTLEST OF DISGUISES, THAT IS TO SAY THE MOST RIDICULOUS, WE HAD TO STAY IN FRONT OF THE MYSTERIOUS DOORWAY DAY AFTER DAY, THROUGH UNEXPECTED DOWNPOURS.
GELATI Paolo Paolini
WHEN THEY WEREN'T ON DUTY, KATZ AND CASTEJON WENT LOOKING TO BUY WEAPONS, AND DIDN'T LET ANYBODY MAKE FUN OF THEM.
CHRIST, KID, IT LOOKS LIKE YOUR STOCK IS AS OLD AND WORN AS OUR ARTERIES!
AH, SO YOU GENTLEMEN ARE CONNOISSEURS. THEN COME THIS WAY...
37

WHILE DI MANNO AND AVIDSEN MET WITH SOME YOUNG TYPES, WHO LAUGHED IN THEIR FACE.

SO WHAT, GRANDDAD... WHY DO YOU THINK WE SHOULD CARE IF SOME FAR-RIGHT OLDIES ARE ACTIVE AGAIN?

AFTER THE EXAMPLE OF MORO'S EXECUTION, IT'S A BIT *LATE* TO GET INTO THE FIELD.

BESIDES, ANYTHING THAT UNDERMINES THE ESTABLISHMENT IS GOOD FOR THE CAUSE. SO WE DON'T CARE ABOUT WHAT MESS YOU'RE IN. FIX IT YOURSELVES.

MEANWHILE, MARIA AND KESSLER READ THE NEWS TO PREDICT THE ATTACK, MOSTLY ARTICLES THAT DIDN'T MAKE THEM LAUGH AT ALL.

I BET THEY'LL ACT DURING A PUBLIC DEMONSTRATION.

ME, I'M LEANING TOWARDS AN ABDUCTION BY CAR.

AS FOR BARSAC AND STRANSKY, THEY ENDEAVORED TO PREPARE THINGS FOR THE NEXT LEG OF THE JOURNEY, WHICH WASN'T GOING TO BE AT ALL FUNNY.

WITH THE LOAD OF SHEEP ON TOP AND YOU UNDERNEATH, WE CAN CROSS ALL OF EUROPE!

SURE, AND DIE OF ASPHYXIA AN HOUR AFTER LEAVING!

ALL THIS TIME, SPRING WAS APPROACHING. IN THE HILLS OF ROME THE SCENT OF MIMOSAS WAS ALMOST TOO STRONG.

STRANGE, THESE GOINGS-ON...

YES, THEY'RE GETTING *READY* FOR SOMETHING.

WHEN THE BLACK ORDER MADE ITS MOVE, IT CAME AS RELIEF, BECAUSE ALL OF US HAD BEEN READY FOR THIS DAY WITHOUT KNOWING WHAT IT WOULD ENTAIL.

WHATEVER YOU DO DON'T LOSE THEM! I'M GOING TO WARN THE OTHERS!

AND HOW DID THE DAY GO, EXACTLY? DIFFICULT TO SAY...

GUERRA! GUER

AN IMPRESSION OF ORDER...

THIS IS IT! TWO LANCIAS AND A FIAT! THEY'RE HEADING FOR DOWNTOWN WITH PAVEL BEHIND THEM.

GREAT! NOW JUMP IN A TAXI AND GET DOWN TO THE PIAZZA DEI FIORI.

...OF CHAOS...

DAMN! THEY'RE GETTING AWAY! I'LL HAVE TO TELEPHONE AGAIN.

...OF ORDER...

DON'T WORRY ABOUT IT, PAVEL! WE'VE FOUND THE SPOT!

THERE'S A MINOR RALLY AT THE PIAZZA DEI FIORI, WITH RENATO TRAVIANI, DEPUTY OF ROME, MEMBER OF THE CENTRAL COMMITTEE, AND MAJOR FIGURE IN THE COMMUNIST PARTY! THAT'S THE PLACE! WE'RE SURE OF IT.

...OF CHAOS...

COME ON, WE'RE GOING!

DAMMIT, I CAN'T FIND THE CLIP!

GET MOVING!

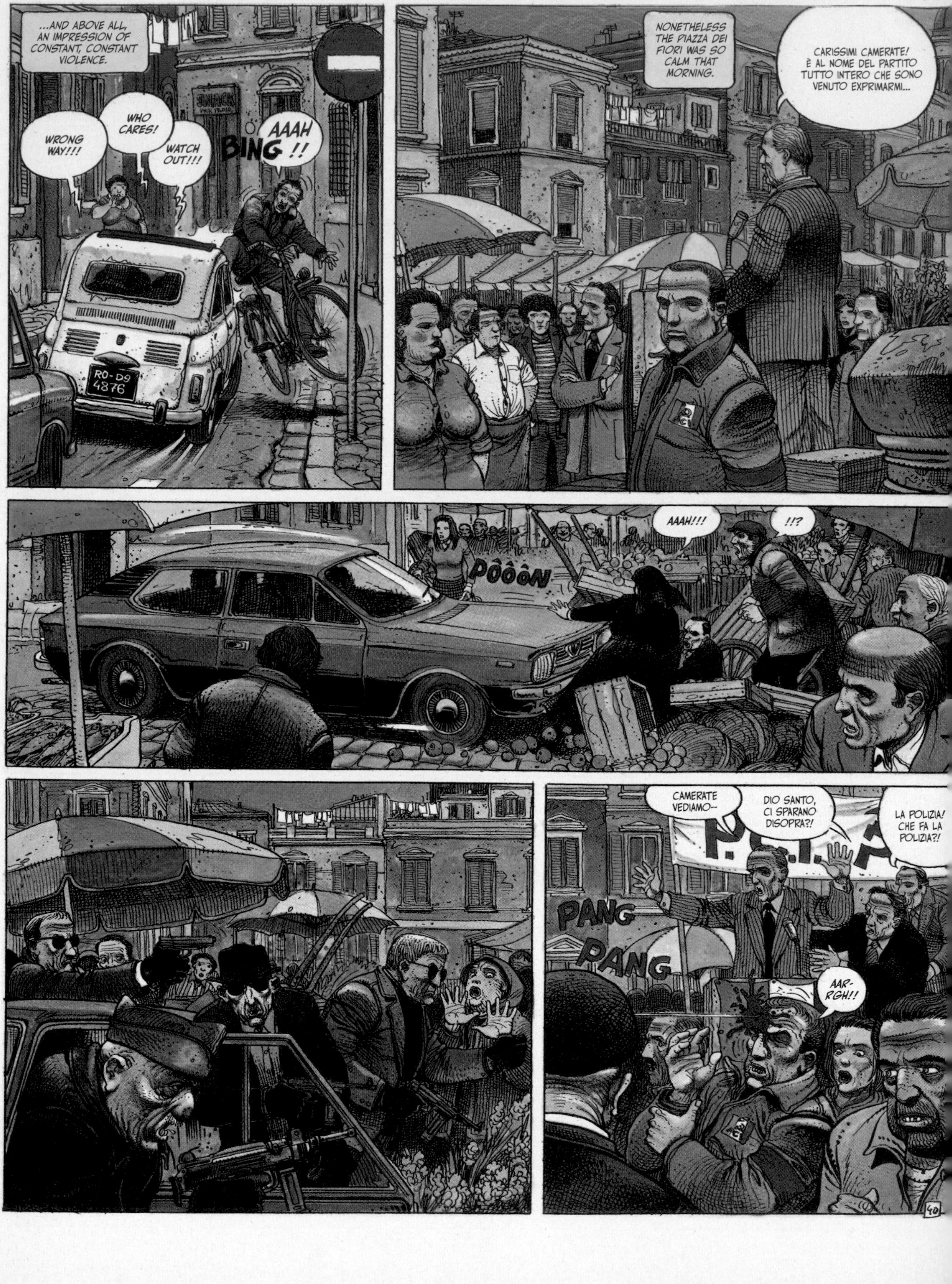
...AND ABOVE ALL, AN IMPRESSION OF CONSTANT, CONSTANT VIOLENCE.
WRONG WAY!!!
WHO CARES!
WATCH OUT!!!
AAAH
BING !!
RO-D9 4876
NONETHELESS THE PIAZZA DEI FIORI WAS SO CALM THAT MORNING.
CARISSIMI CAMERATE! È AL NOME DEL PARTITO TUTTO INTERO CHE SONO VENUTO EXPRIMARMI...
PÔÔÔN
AAAH!!!
!!?
CAMERATE VEDIAMO--
DIO SANTO, CI SPARANO DISOPRA?!
LA POLIZIA! CHE FA LA POLIZIA?!
PANG
PANG
AAR-RGH!!

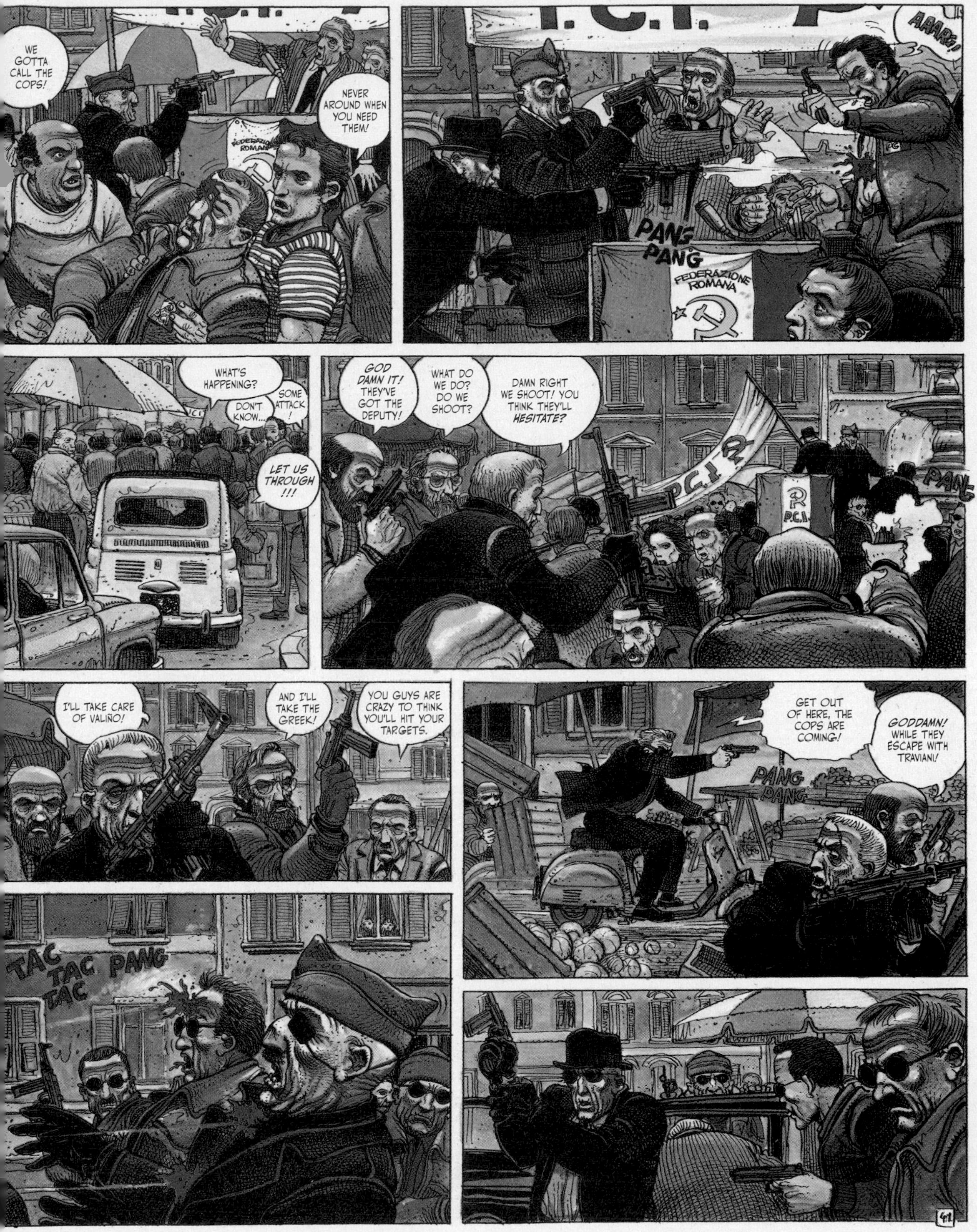

WE GOTTA CALL THE COPS!
NEVER AROUND WHEN YOU NEED THEM!
P.C.I.
AAARG!
PANG PANG
FEDERAZIONE ROMANA
WHAT'S HAPPENING?
DON'T KNOW...
SOME ATTACK!
LET US THROUGH!!!
GOD DAMN IT! THEY'VE GOT THE DEPUTY!
WHAT DO WE DO? DO WE SHOOT?
DAMN RIGHT WE SHOOT! YOU THINK THEY'LL HESITATE?
P.C.I.
PANG
I'LL TAKE CARE OF VALIÑO!
AND I'LL TAKE THE GREEK!
YOU GUYS ARE CRAZY TO THINK YOU'LL HIT YOUR TARGETS.
GET OUT OF HERE, THE COPS ARE COMING!
GODDAMN! WHILE THEY ESCAPE WITH TRAVIANI!
PANG PANG
TAC TAC TAC PANG
41

OH, SHIT!!!

PAVEL!!!

HERE'S THE COPS!

DAMN QUICK TOO.

HEY, YOU THERE!

WE'RE THE ONES WHO ARE GOING TO PAY FOR IT...

EVERYBODY INTO THE CARS! WE'VE GOT TO SEPARATE!

MEET TONIGHT AT THE APPOINTED PLACE!

AAAGH...

P.C.I.

YOU OKAY, PAVEL?

QUICK MARIA, WE'VE GOT TO GET AWAY. THE COPS...

DID YOU SEE THAT? THEY MANAGED TO PICK UP GENERAL VALIÑO.

OKAY, WE'LL FOLLOW THEM!

WOW, YOU'RE DRIVING JUST LIKE A YOUNG MAN, PAVEL!!!

LIKE THE OLD LUNATIC THAT I AM, YOU MEAN! IT'S GOING TO BE HARD TO KEEP ON THEIR TAIL.

WE'RE HEADING OUT OF ROME.

AT LEAST THEY HAVEN'T SPOTTED US.

WE'RE ON THE ROAD TO CASSIA.

HEY, THEY'RE TURNING IN.

LOOKS LIKE A CONVENT.

YES, THE PERPETUAL ADORATION OF THE HOLY SHROUD! BUT I ALSO HEARD AN OLD COUNTESS TALKING ABOUT A VERY PRIVATE CLINIC AT THE BACK OF THE GARDEN WHERE THE EXTREMELY WEALTHY GO TO MEND THEMSELVES.

WELL, WELL, I BELIEVE I HAVE A PROPOSAL TO MAKE TONIGHT, THEN...

INDEED, THAT NIGHT, AFTER AN EXHAUSTING DAY OF LAYING LOW, IT WAS THE TIME FOR PROPOSALS.

KESSLER, AT LAST!!!

WHEW... TODAY WAS HARD. IS EVERYONE HERE?

YES, BY SOME MIRACLE! THANKS TO OUR LUCK, THE POLICE AREN'T TALKING ABOUT ANYONE ELSE BUT US!

THAT'S IT! THE BLACK ORDER BRIGADE JUST CLAIMED RESPONSIBILITY FOR THE ATTACK AND ARE DEMANDING A BILLION-LIRA RANSOM!

IF THE COMMUNIST PARTY'S AS LOW ON FUNDS AS THEY CLAIM, COMRADE TRAVIANI IS IN TROUBLE.

IN ANY CASE IT'S TIME TO START THINKING ABOUT LEAVING THE COUNTRY QUICKLY. WE WON'T EVADE THE NET THEY'RE PUTTING IN PLACE FOR MUCH LONGER.

I'VE FOUND AN OLD ARMY PILOT WHO'S PREPARED TO FLY US OUT DISCREETLY IN EXCHANGE FOR THE LAST SCRAPINGS OF DONAHUE'S LEGACY.

YES, BUT WHERE TO?

QUITE SO...NOW, WE'RE THE ONLY ONES WHO KNOW WHERE THAT BASTARD VALIÑO IS. IF HE'S STILL ALIVE WE HAVE TO MAKE HIM TALK SO WE CAN FIND OUT WHERE THE BLACK ORDER TOOK THE DEPUTY.

AS COWARDLY AS HE IS CRUEL, GENERAL VALIÑO. THAT'S WHAT THEY SAID DURING THE GUERRA CIVIL.

WHAT A GOOD IDEA...TORTURING THE TORTURER.

I HOPE YOU HAVE SOME EXTRA CASSOCKS, FATHER CASTEJON, BECAUSE HERE'S MY PLAN...

AT THE CONVENT, SURROUNDED BY LAUREL TREES RUSTLING IN THE BREEZE, THINGS HAPPENED QUICKLY.

DON'T COUNT ON ME FOR THIS DIRTY BUSINESS.

ME, I'M GAME.

IF WE COULD JUST SEIZE THE INITIATIVE, WE COULD TURN THINGS AROUND.

DO YOU HAVE AN *AUTHORIZATION*, MY BROTHERS?

BUT OF COURSE WE DO, BROTHER.

HERE IT IS... ...MY BROTHER!

BING

GET DOWN.

?!

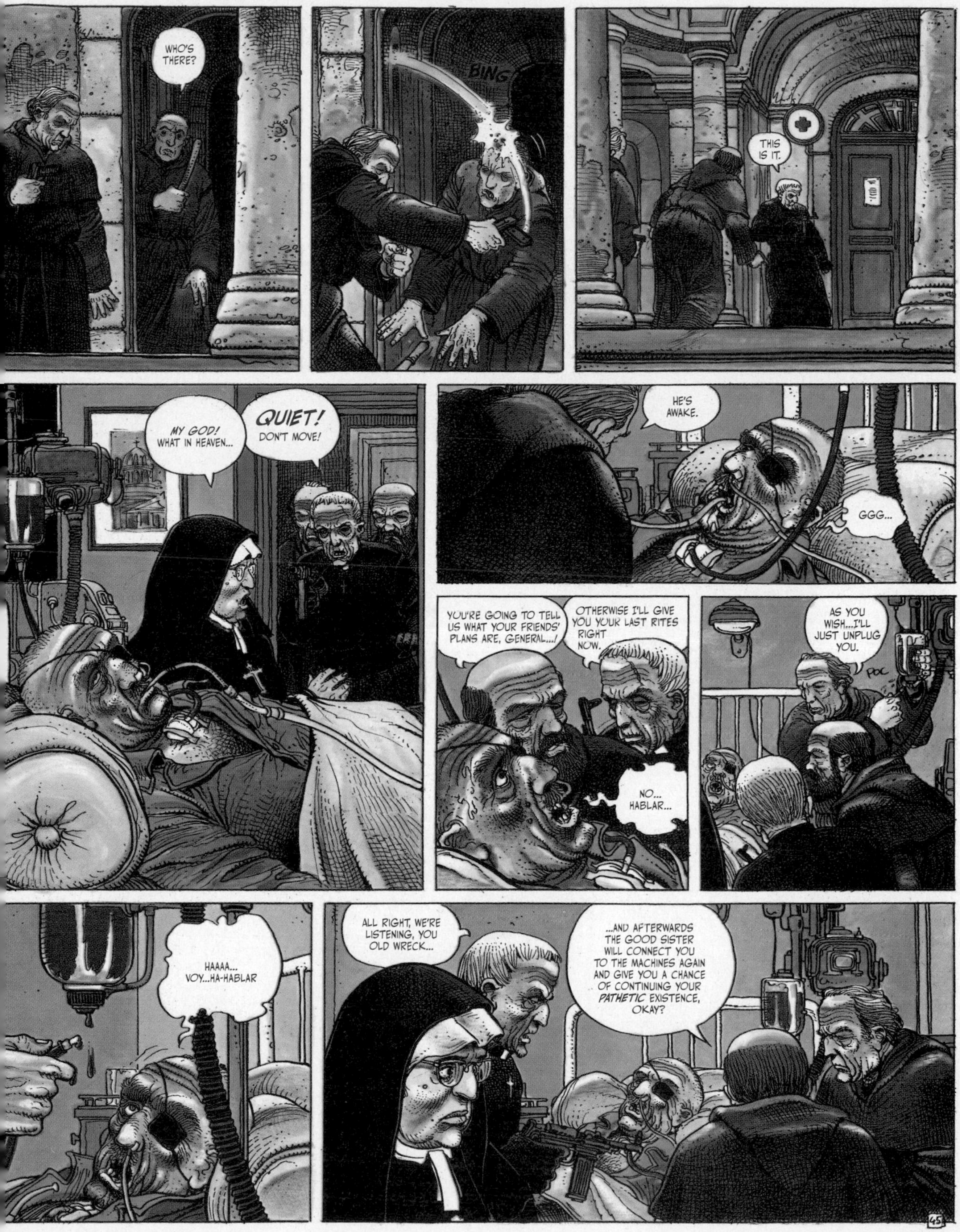
WHO'S THERE?
BING
THIS IS IT.
MY GOD! WHAT IN HEAVEN...
QUIET! DON'T MOVE!
HE'S AWAKE.
GGG...
YOU'RE GOING TO TELL US WHAT YOUR FRIENDS' PLANS ARE, GENERAL...!
OTHERWISE I'LL GIVE YOU YOUR LAST RITES RIGHT NOW.
NO... HABLAR...
AS YOU WISH...I'LL JUST UNPLUG YOU.
POC
HAAAA... VOY...HA-HABLAR
ALL RIGHT, WE'RE LISTENING, YOU OLD WRECK...
...AND AFTERWARDS THE GOOD SISTER WILL CONNECT YOU TO THE MACHINES AGAIN AND GIVE YOU A CHANCE OF CONTINUING YOUR *PATHETIC* EXISTENCE, OKAY?
45

AND AS DAYLIGHT CRESTED THE HILLS, NEAR A TINY AIRFIELD WELL-HIDDEN BY CYPRESS TREES...

HERE COME OUR THREE TORTURERS.

YES...

AND?

WE'RE OFF TO SWITZERLAND.

WHAT DID HE SAY EXACTLY?

NOT VERY MUCH... HE PASSED OUT FROM FRIGHT AND NEVER HAD TIME TO TELL US WHERE THE BLACK ORDER WAS EXACTLY.

THE ONLY THING FOR CERTAIN IS THAT, DESPITE VARIOUS ANONYMOUS DONATIONS, THEY NEED MONEY TOO. THE RANSOM WILL BE PAID THROUGH GENEVA, WHERE THE ORDER HAS STRONG BANKING CONNECTIONS.

THAT WAY THEY CAN KILL TWO BIRDS WITH ONE STONE: DISCREDIT THE COMMUNISTS AND REFILL THEIR COFFERS.

LET'S HURRY. WE HAVE TO LEAVE BEFORE SUNRISE.

IF THEY PAY...

BAH...

YES, AS THE PALE SPRINGTIME SUN ROSE ABOVE THE CALM TUSCANY VALLEY, OUR JOURNEY CONTINUED, EACH ONE OF US TRYING TO BELIEVE THAT WE HAD A PURPOSE.

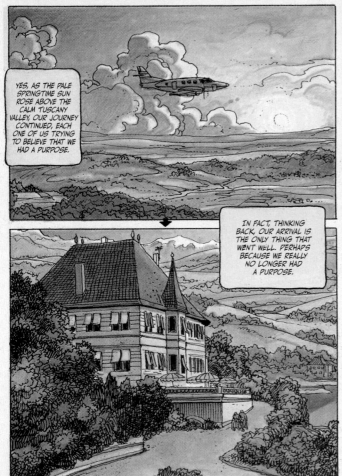

IN FACT, THINKING BACK, OUR ARRIVAL IS THE ONLY THING THAT WENT WELL. PERHAPS BECAUSE WE REALLY NO LONGER HAD A PURPOSE.

OUR ARRIVAL SWITZERLAND W WITHOUT A HI AND THE OLD F HOME ON T SHORES OF L GENEVA WHERE ALL HOLED SEEMED PERF FOR A BUNCH WORN-OUT O WAR-HORSES

PERHAPS BECAUSE O WILL WAS ERODED THE SIGHT OF TH DECREPITUDE OF T OTHER OLD DOTAR SPENDING THE DA STARING OUT UPO A LAKE AS CLOUDE AS THEIR EYES?

EVEN THE CLUMSY ANTICS OF SCIENTIFIC "SOCIALISM" DIDN'T MAKE ANY OF US LAUGH.

THE GENERAL SECRETARIES OF THE EUROPEAN COMMUNIST PARTIES GATHERED TODAY IN PARIS. AFTER REJECTING, ACCORDING TO RELIABLE SOURCES, AN OFFER OF FINANCIAL ASSISTANCE FROM COMECON, THEY ARE CONTEMPLATING TAKING UP AN INTERNATIONAL COLLECTION TO PAY THE RANSOM FOR DEPUTY TRAVIANI, NOW KIDNAPPED THREE DAYS AGO. BUT OTHER MORE DISCREET MEANS MAY...

THINK THEY'LL COUGH UP, MARIA?

I DON'T CARE.

WHILE WAITING FOR THINGS TO GET STARTED AGAIN, THE FORCED INACTIVITY MADE OUR BRAINS START WORKING ALMOST IN SPITE OF THEMSELVES.

LOOK, ANOTHER ARTICLE ON THE BLACK ORDER BRIGADE. NOT VERY WELL-INFORMED, BUT IT'S STILL GOOD NEWS IF IT GETS THE POLICE AFTER THEM.

YEAH, EXCEPT I'VE JUST READ ONE ON US. JUST AS POORLY INFORMED, BUT STILL BAD NEWS. AND FOR THE SAME REASONS, IF YOU TAKE MY MEANING...

HMM...IN DENMARK, THEY'RE STILL CONCERNED ABOUT THE DISAPPEARANCE OF THE MINISTER AVIDSEN.

LUCKY DEVIL...

YEAH, RIGHT.

WHEREAS MY NEWSPAPER DOESN'T EVEN SEEM TO NOTICE I'M GONE. TOO BAD...

AND I HAVE THE STRANGE IMPRESSION THAT PHILOSOPHICAL THOUGHT IN GERMANY CONTINUES TO ADVANCE *WITHOUT* ME.

REALLY! YOU KNOW YOU'RE ALL SERIOUSLY STARTING TO GET ON MY NERVES, YOU BUNCH OF HAS-BEENS!?!

AS FOR ME, I'M A WOMAN, AND I STILL HAVE A TASTE FOR LIFE.

YEAH, WE ALL MEAN VERY LITTLE, BUT ESPECIALLY IN THE SPY GAME, WHERE ONE MISSING MAN MORE OR LESS...

AT OUR AGE WE HAVE TO START GETTING USED TO THE IDEA OF RETURNING TO OBLIVION.

SO IF YOU GUYS WANT TO SIT HERE RETURNING TO OBLIVION WHILE DREAMING ABOUT MAKING MINOR CHANGES TO HISTORY IN THE MIDDLE OF AN OLD FOLKS' HOME, GO RIGHT AHEAD! BUT NOT ME! *SEE YOU LATER!!!*

BUT, MARIA!?

HOLY GOD!

WHAT A WOMAN!

WHAT CLASS!

WELL, SINCE THAT'S HOW IT IS, I'M OFF TO FIND A DISCREET BORDELLO IN GENEVA. AFTER YEARS OF IMPOSED ABSTINENCE, I'M SURE THE LORD WILL BE UNDERSTANDING.

PERHAPS IF I COULD FIND A COMFORTABLE BAR, WITH LEATHER SOFAS AND RARE LIQUOR...

MARIA HAS A POINT. WE'RE ONLY LETTING TIME SLIP BY...I'M GOING TO GO RENT A BOAT. I ALWAYS HOPED THAT I WOULD CATCH AT LEAST ONE FISH BEFORE I DIED.

INDEED!

PUFF PUFF

WE HAVE FINE TASTES.

OUR DEAR COMRADES MAKE ME LAUGH WITH THEIR TASTE FOR LUXURY... RECREATIONAL BOATING, CALL-GIRLS, AND FINE LIQUEURS, I ASK YOU! WE DON'T HAVE A CENT LEFT!

AND IF I TRIED TO MAKE CONTACT WITH THE NETWORK OF EXILES THAT I KNOW IN SWITZERLAND...?

NOW THAT'S AN IDEA. WHEN ALL'S SAID AND DONE, I ALSO HAVE A NUMBER OF CONTACTS IN THE REVOLVING HUB OF NETWORKS IN THIS SCENIC DEMOCRATIC COUNTRY.

MMM... SINCE AT THE MOMENT NOBODY KNOWS WHERE WE'RE GOING, GO AHEAD IF YOU CAN DO IT WITH CAUTION. BUT THAT DOESN'T RESOLVE OUR FINANCIAL PROBLEMS AT ALL.

JUST A MINUTE! IF YOU ALLOW ME TO DIP INTO THE FUNDS TO BUY A NICE SUIT AND GO TO A GOOD HAIRDRESSER, I MIGHT HAVE A CUSHY JOB.

WHAT KIND?

OH, JUST A HARMLESS LITTLE ANNOUNCEMENT IN THE "FINANCIAL TIMES."

BUT FOR THOSE WHO CAN READ BETWEEN THE LINES, I BELIEVE THEY'RE LOOKING FOR A TRAVELING BANKER.

AND WHAT'S THAT?

YES, TELL US ABOUT IT...

OH, MY COMRADES, I SEE THAT IT'S POSSIBLE FOR THE OLD ANTI-IMPERIALIST VANGUARD, BOLDLY BATTLING THE GREAT MASS OF INTERNATIONAL CAPITAL, TO BE UNAWARE OF A FEW THINGS.

ALRIGHT, SO WE HAVEN'T ALL BEEN INVOLVED IN UPPER-LEVEL BOURGEOIS POLITICS.

WELL NOW, WOULD YOU BELIEVE IT'S JUST A SMALL JOB, CONSISTING, FOR EXAMPLE, OF GAMBLING ON CURRENCY DEVALUATIONS AND MOVEMENTS OF THE STOCK MARKET... AND, UM...OF CARRYING MONEY INTO OTHER COUNTRIES...TO KEEP THINGS BALANCED, AS THEY SAY...

WORK INVOLVING UTMOST DISCRETION, IT MUST BE SAID, WITH VERY, VERY LARGE COMMISSIONS.

I SEE.

MMMM...

SO WHAT DO YOU SAY?

I'LL TAKE YOU TO AN ENGLISH TAILOR I USED TO KNOW.

AS FOR ME, I WAS A BARBER AT MY CONCENTRATION CAMP BUT I THINK YOU NEED SOMETHING A LITTLE MORE *RESPECTABLE*.

THE WEATHER BECAME FINE AND FRESH OVER THE LAKE. OCCASIONALLY, BIRDS WOULD SKIM THE SILVERY SURFACE OF THE WATER.

DI MANNO STILL HADN'T CAUGHT ANYTHING, AND SPENT WHOLE DAYS IN HIS BOAT, STARING AT HIS MOTIONLESS LURE.

CASTEJON WAS SULLEN AND GRUMBLED THAT HE WAS PAST THE AGE OF HAVING TO ASK FOR POCKET MONEY TO GO INTO TOWN.

BARSAC TOOK LONG WALKS IN THE COUNTRY AND TOLD TALES OF TREES IN BLOOM, WHICH NOBODY LISTENED TO.

MARIA HAD DISAPPEARED, BUT A PICTURE OF HER CHATTING IN THE MIDDLE OF A GROUP OF YOUNG ARTISTS WAS PUBLISHED IN THE PAPER, AND IT LOOKED LIKE SHE WAS HAVING FUN.

49

KESSLER READ THICK BOOKS THROUGHOUT THE DAY AND TALKED ABOUT RECOMMENCING WORK ON HIS EPISTEMOLOGY THESIS, BUT NOBODY LISTENED TO HIM EITHER.

THE NEWS ALMOST NEVER MENTIONED THE DEPUTY TRAVIANI ANY MORE, WHICH MEANT THAT THE NEGOTIATIONS WERE GOING WELL.

IN ITALY, IT'S THE TWENTY-THIRD ROUND OF THE ELECTIONS.

OLD VALIÑO DIED WITHOUT A FUSS AND ONLY MADRID'S "ABC" ANNOUNCED THE NEWS, ON PAGE THIRTEEN.

AVIDSEN, CARRYING PRETTY FAWN-COLORED LEATHER BRIEFCASES, MADE REPEATED TRIPS BETWEEN FRANCE AND SWITZERLAND WITH A SCHEDULE SO FRENZIED THAT IT HARDLY LEFT HIM THE TIME TO BRING US A FEW TIDY SUMS OF MONEY.

REMEMBER TO GET THE PHOTOS I ASKED FOR.

DON'T WORRY!

BUT FINALLY ONE EVENING, KATZ AND STRANSKY RETURNED IN A HAPPY MOOD.

I'VE GOT A LEAD.

ME TOO...

AHA, THINGS ARE MOVING AGAIN.

I BELIEVE I KNOW WHERE THEIR HIDEOUT IS.

SOME VERBENA?

AND I THINK I'VE UNCOVERED HOW THE RANSOM IS TO BE PAID.

IN FACT, IT WAS A YUGOSLAVIAN FRIEND, WHO SOMETIMES WORKS AS A BODYGUARD, WHO TOLD ME ABOUT SOME KIND OF ROCOCO CASTLE IN THE MOUNTAINS NEAR THE ITALIAN BORDER. IT HAS A SKATING RINK THAT VERY MUCH LOOKS LIKE A LANDING PAD FOR HELICOPTERS, LOOKOUT POSTS DISGUISED AS CLIMBERS' HUTS, DEER HUNTERS CARRYING MAUSERS. YOU GET THE IDEA...

I HAVE A...UM...RELIABLE CORRESPONDENT WHO WORKS IN THE BANK. WELL, WOULD YOU BELIEVE THAT AN ORDINARILY VERY STABLE FIRM, INTERNATIONALLY KNOWN FOR ITS SECRET NUMBERED ACCOUNTS, IS UNDERGOING A FLURRY OF ACTIVITY? IT'S CALLED THE CREDIT MEDITERRANEAN.

TAKE ACTION...WHAT ELSE COULD WE DO NOW? BESIDES, WOULDN'T IT BE BETTER THAN JUST THINKING? THE DAY AFTER, WE WERE AT BATTLE STATIONS.

I'LL BE STAYING HERE. I STILL HAVEN'T CAUGHT ANYTHING.

AS YOU PREFER, MY FRIEND.

ALL VERY INTERESTING. AT LAST WE CAN TAKE ACTION!

BUT THE CASTLE LOOKED A LOT LIKE A FORTRESS.

HUFF... I CAN'T GO ON.

HAND ME THE BINOCULARS, PRITCH.

WHAT A PLACE!

TO THINK THOSE BASTARDS JUST TRAVEL BY HELICOPTER.

SO DID THE BANK, AS WELL.

WHAT COULD BE GOING ON BEHIND THOSE WALLS?

MY FRIEND, ONLY GOD AND THE INTERNATIONAL COMMUNIST PARTY KNOW FOR SURE.

WE HAD TO MAKE A PLAN. OR SO WE ALL THOUGHT...

WE'D NEED CANNONS TO TAKE THAT CASTLE!

AND MORTARS TO GET INTO THAT BANK!

YEAH.

BUT LIFE, AS USUAL, TOOK CARE OF UNDOING ALL OUR PLANS.

PFFF... ME, I'M GLAD TO BE BACK.

WE'RE BECOMING LIKE THOSE RETIREES.

MAYBE SO, BUT MOUNTAIN CLIMBING IS NO LONGER OUR...

HEY, LOOK, WHAT'S ALL THE COMMOTION ABOUT?

LIFE...AND DEATH...

AH, GENTLEMEN...

WHAT'S HAPPENING?

AHEM...YOUR ITALIAN FRIEND...

YES, THIS AFTERNOON ON THE LAKE...

...THE POOR MAN. HE HAD A STROKE.

DI MANNO! SWEET JESUS...

HE'D JUST CAUGHT A PERCH WHEN...

I COULD SEE HIM CLEARLY! HE LET OUT A TERRIBLE SHOUT, THEN WHAM!

WAS IT A GOOD-SIZED PERCH, AT LEAST?

OH, THIS IS IT...

MY DEAR OLD FRIEND, YOU FINALLY CAUGHT YOUR FISH.

WE LET THE POLICE KNOW RIGHT AWAY.

THEY SAID THAT, IN FACT, THEY HAD BEEN WAITING TO TALK TO YOU.

WHAT!?

DAMN, THAT'S ALL WE NEEDED!

HURRY, COMRADES! WE'RE GETTING OUT!!!

BUT!?

HEY, YOU THERE!

WHAT HAPPENED AFTER THE LONG AND ALL-TOO-CALM DAYS BY LAKE GENEVA IS NOW A BLUR.

TURN ON THE RADIO!

AFTER A SUSPICIOUS DEATH THAT TOOK PLACE THIS AFTERNOON, A MASSIVE POLICE OPERATION HAS BEEN SET IN MOTION AGAINST A SMALL GROUP OF UNKNOWNS, WHO THE POLICE SUSPECT ARE TIED TO THE TRAVIANI AFFAIR. ROADBLOCKS ARE...

IN THE BEGINNING, THE LARGE CAR DROVE WITHOUT DIRECTION OVER THE TINY MOUNTAIN ROADS.

THOSE BASTARDS!

JUST WAIT, WE'LL BE THE ONES TO TAKE THE BLAME.

AND THEN STRANSKY REMEMBERED AN AUTONOMOUS GROUP HE KNEW IN THE SWISS MOUNTAINS.

AND MEANWHILE...

YEAH, THE BLACK ORDER WILL BE HAVING A GOOD LAUGH.

TURN LEFT HERE, QUICKLY!

AND NOW FOR OUR TOP STORY THIS EVENING. THE DEPUTY TRAVIANI WAS RECOVERED SAFE AND SOUND IN AN ISOLATED SPOT IN THE ITALIAN ALPS.

THERE GOES THAT!

IT WAS THERE, TWO DAYS LATER, WITH THE TELEVISION BLARING AMONG TURKISH WORKERS SILENTLY EATING THEIR BEANS, THAT THE NEWS HIT US.

EKMEK?

BY NIGHTFALL, WE HAD FOUND SHELTER IN A CAMP FOR IMMIGRANT WORKERS, ACCUSTOMED TO BEING SURPRISED BY NOTHING...

BE ALRIGHT?

WE'LL MAKE DO.

WE'LL GET RID OF THE CAR FOR YOU.

THANKS FOR EVERYTHING, GUYS...

53

A HIDING PLACE SUSPECTED TO HAVE BEEN USED BY THE KIDNAPPERS WAS DESERTED.

DESERTED?!!

WHAT DO YOU KNOW...

ŞARAP?

ÇOK, THANK YOU.

IT IS NOT KNOWN WHERE, WHEN, OR EVEN WHETHER THE RANSOM WAS PAID. AT PRESENT, THE ITALIAN COMMUNIST PARTY IS REFUSING TO COMMENT. SWISS BANKING AGENCIES DON'T KNOW ANYTHING ABOUT IT.

VERY ELEGANTLY DONE!!!

THE MAN WHO DIED ON LAKE GENEVA HAS BEEN IDENTIFIED. GIANCARLO DI MANNO, THE MINOR ITALIAN JUDGE WHO WAS BURIED THIS AFTERNOON, WAS ALSO A A FORMER MEMBER OF THE INTERNATIONAL BRIGADES, AND HIS TIES TO THE EXTREME LEFT HAVE NOW BEEN CONFIRMED.

POOR OLD MAN! BURIED ALONE IN THE DIRT, LIKE A DOG. WHAT A PITY.

I PRAY FOR HIM.

BAH...

MEANWHILE, INVESTIGATIONS CONTINUE WITH HOPES OF FINDING A GROUP THAT COULD BE SIGNING THEIR ATTACKS IN THE NAME OF THE BLACK ORDER, IN ORDER TO THROW SUSPICION ONTO THE EXTREME RIGHT.

HA HA... SEE THERE, HOW TALENTED THE SWISS POLICE CAN BE.

TALENTED AT THROWING UP A SMOKE SCREEN, SURE...

WE'RE UP TO OUR NECKS IN HOT WATER NOW.

TOO TRUE.

AND MY TURKISH FRIENDS DON'T WANT US TO TAKE ANY ACTION AT ALL. TOO RISKY FOR THEM.

WHAT DO YOU MEAN, YOU'VE BEEN EXPECTING OUR CALL?

YES, YES... DON'T MOVE. I'M COMING WITH MARIA AND WE'LL PICK YOU UP.

TELEPHO

WE HAVE TO CONTACT AVIDSEN!

MMM...HE LEFT ME A NUMBER...A SECURE ONE, APPARENTLY...

LET'S TRY IT. HE'S THE ONLY ONE WHO CAN GET US OUT OF HERE.

54

WHAT HAPPENED AFTER THAT IS INDEED A BLUR. EVERYTHING STARTED MOVING TOO FAST.

BUT MARIA, WHAT ARE YOU DOING HERE?

I'D LIKE YOU ALL TO MEET MY NEW BOYFRIEND, VICTOR. HE'S A FILMMAKER.

AND AVIDSEN, HOW DID YOU DO IT?

I'LL EXPLAIN LATER. THE BORDERS ARE SEALED, BUT VICTOR HAS AN AUTHORIZATION FROM SWISS TELEVISION TO SHOOT IN GERMANY. YOU GUYS WILL BE THE TECHNICAL CREW.

AS FAR AS THE BORDER, ANYWAY, BECAUSE THE REAL CREW WENT BY PLANE YESTERDAY.

I SEE...

WE SHOULD GET GOING.

HERE ARE FAKE DOCUMENTS WITH YOUR PHOTOS, MY FRIENDS. DONE BY AN EXPERT, AS YOU CAN SEE.

YOU DIDN'T WASTE ANY TIME.

AH, BEING A TRAVELING BANKER IS LIKE BEING A MINISTER. IT'S A GOOD JOB IF YOU DON'T DO IT FOR TOO LONG. INSTEAD OF DELIVERING MY LAST SUITCASE, I STARTED PUTTING IT TO GOOD USE, AS YOU CAN SEE...

AND MARIA?

WHEN I CALLED HER, SHE HAD ALREADY WORKED EVERYTHING OUT AND MADE PREPARATIONS.

QUIET BACK THERE!

CALM DOWN, VICTOR DEAR, THESE POLICE LOOK REASSURINGLY STUPID TO ME.

WELL, HERE WE ARE!

YEAH, IT'S STRANGE TO RETURN TO MY COUNTRY LIKE THIS.

FAREWELL, YOU OLD BUNGLERS. THIS TIME I'M AFRAID WE WON'T BE SEEING EACH OTHER AGAIN.

FAREWELL, MARIA.

ALL THE BEST, MY FRIEND.

TAKE CARE OF YOURSELF, BARSAC, AND TRY TO COOL THEIR PASSIONS A BIT.

UH... MARIA...WE HAVE TO GO.

HAH, HER YOUNG FLAME WON'T LAST LONG. THAT BOY DOESN'T HAVE ENOUGH BALLS FOR HER.

YOU'RE GETTING LEWD IN YOUR OLD AGE, CASTEJON, IF YOU DON'T MIND ME SAYING.

TO START WITH, I SUGGEST WE WALK TOWARDS THE CHARMING AND TYPICAL VILLAGE WE SEE DOWN THERE...

NOT MUCH CHOICE, ANYWAY.

EVERYTHING HAPPENED FAST, THINGS GOING TOO WELL OR TOO BADLY FOR IT EVEN TO MATTER.

WHAT THE HELL ARE WE DOING HERE?

I DON'T THINK WE'RE REALLY CERTAIN.

MY ACHING FEET...

SO, PRITCH, COULD IT BE THAT YOU WANT TO GIVE THIS UP?

OF COURSE NOT, BUT...

YOU'RE GETTING *SOFT* IN YOUR OLD AGE, PRITCHARD, IF YOU DON'T MIND ME SAYING.

BRINGEN SIE UNS BITTE EINE FLASCHE MOSELWEIN...

BITTE...

LISTEN, I'M NOT WITHOUT CONTACTS, IN THE UNIVERSITIES AND OTHER PLACES.

IF YOU GIVE ME SOME TIME, I'M SURE I CAN UNCOVER THE BLACK ORDER'S TRAIL. WHAT DO YOU SAY?

AND YOUR THESIS ON EPISTEMOLOGY?

TOO BAD FOR EPISTEMOLOGY. I'LL ALWAYS HAVE TIME TO WRITE IT LATER.

DO YOU HAVE ANY MONEY LEFT, AVIDSEN?

PLENTY. AND IT HAPPENS TO BE IN DEUTSCHE MARKS.

BUT NOT MUCH TIME WAS LEFT FOR HANS KESSLER, EMINENT PHILOSOPHER AND PROFESSOR AT HEIDELBERG UNIVERSITY.

WONDERFUL. WE CAN RENT A CAR!

BUT HE DIDN'T KNOW THAT AS HE SET OFF ON HIS PECULIAR QUEST.

WHERE TO?

FIRST, BAVARIA...

HOWEVER, AFTER A SERIES OF MEETINGS, IT ALL BECAME MURKY, AND THE BLACK ORDER SUDDENLY SEEMED UNREAL THROUGH THE SMOKE OF THE BEER CELLARS.

NOBODY HAD HEARD ANYTHING. NOBODY EVEN SEEMED INTERESTED.

SUMMER HAD ARRIVED, AND, IN THE THICK HEAT OF THE CITY, A TYPE OF NUMBNESS SEEMED TO PENETRATE OUR WEARY BODIES.

WHAT IMPRESSION DID THE FORGOTTEN SURVIVORS OF FORGOTTEN BRIGADES MAKE ON THE YOUNG CROWD, WITH THEIR LIVELY WITS AND STEADY HANDS? NOT MUCH OF ONE, CERTAINLY.

57

AND AS FRANKFURT FOLLOWED MUNICH, WHAT IMPRESSION WAS MADE ON THE OLD MEN WITH DROOPING FLESH BY THE YOUNG GIRLS WITH SUPPLE BODIES WHO SPOKE OF GENTLE TACTICS AND NON-REPRESSIVE REGIMES? NOT MUCH OF ONE EITHER, PROBABLY...

TWO LINES OF ACTION, TWO BASTIONS OF HOPE, AND MANY CRUEL PIECES OF HISTORY, ALL INTERSECTING WHERE NEITHER SIDE HAD MUCH TO SAY TO THE OTHER.

BUT IT COULDN'T BE DENIED THAT KESSLER, THROUGH EPISTEMOLOGY OR THROUGH OTHER THINGS, HAD A WHOLE LOT OF CONTACTS, AND, ONE FINE DAY, SOMEWHERE ON THE BANKS OF THE RHINE, IT ALL CAME TOGETHER.

LOTTE, I'M SO *HAPPY* TO SEE YOU!

ME TOO, PROFESSOR!

IT WAS ONE OF HIS FORMER STUDENTS, NOW A FREE-LANCE JOURNALIST FOR THE EXTREME LEFT, WHO PUT US BACK ON COURSE.

BUT I'M TELLING YOU IT'S TRUE...A GUY I INTERVIEWED ALMOST BY CHANCE TOLD ME ABOUT IT IN ORDER TO SHOW OFF. I DIDN'T PAY MUCH ATTENTION AT THE TIME.

AND NOW, JUST TWO DAYS AGO, WHEN I BECAME SURE HE REALLY WAS A MEMBER OF THE VIKING JUGEND...

AND WHAT'S THAT?

A SMALL AND LITTLE KNOWN, BUT ACTIVE NEO-NAZI GROUP.

IT WAS THE VIKING JUGEND THAT HID YOUR OLD MEN WHEN THEY CROSSED OVER INTO GERMANY, I'M SURE OF IT. THEY ARRIVED BY HELICOPTER IN THE SUBURBS AROUND HAMBURG.

HMM... THAT COULD FIT.

AND NOW THEY'RE PLANNING SOMETHING BIG IN HOLLAND WITH YOUNG GUYS LIKE THE BASTARD THAT I EVEN HAD TO SLEEP WITH JUST TO GET SOME INFORMATION OUT OF HIM.

WELL, *HAPPY* TO BE BACK IN ACTION, CASTEJON?

OH YES, DEFINITELY !!!

AND YOU, STRANSKY?

PFE...

60

ME, I'M NOT UPSET TO BE LEAVING THIS COUNTRY. TOO MANY UNPLEASANT FAMILY MEMORIES...

I WANT TO LEAVE, TOO. AND SINCE I FINALLY HAVE A SCOOP I MIGHT AS WELL MAKE THE MOST OUT OF IT BY STAYING WITH YOU GUYS.

AND YOUR YOUNG VIKING?

I DUMPED THE *BASTARD* YESTERDAY, THANK GOD.

KESSLER WAS HAPPY AND WE WEREN'T TOO SURE WHETHER IT WAS BECAUSE HE HAD DELIVERED AS PROMISED OR BECAUSE LOTTE'S SMILE WARMED HIS OLD BONES.

BUT HE DIDN'T STAY HAPPY FOR LONG, BECAUSE, JUST AS WE NEARED THE DUTCH BORDER...

SHALL WE TAKE A WALK AND STRETCH OUR LEGS?

SURE, PROFESSOR!

IT MIGHT BE A FLASHY TRUCK BUT IT SURE IS UNCOMFORTABLE.

SAY, WHAT DO YOU SUPPOSE...?!!!

elektro GHZ

EVERYBODY DOWN!!!

59

AAAAH!

KESSLER!!!

BRATATATATAC

Wur
AUS

OH, LORD...

DEAD...BOTH OF THEM...

I CAN'T TAKE ANY MORE OF THIS!!! IT'S TOO AWFUL.

KESSLER, GOOD OLD KESSLER!!!

BE BRAVE, COMRADES... WE MUST GO ON. NOW MORE THAN EVER.

THAT'S RIGHT, PRITCH. KEEP US TOGETHER.

SURE, GO ON! BUT WHERE, DAMMIT?! WHERE!

CALM DOWN, PAVEL!

GO ON TO HOLLAND, FOR EXAMPLE...

WE GO ON TILL THE VERY END, AND YOU ALL KNOW IT.

YOU THINK IT WAS THE BLACK ORDER THAT MADE THE ATTACK, KATZ?

I'D BE SURPRISED IF IT WAS, BECAUSE THEY WOULDN'T HAVE MISSED US. THAT YOUNG GIRL MUST JUST HAVE BEEN FOLLOWED BY HER VIKING FRIEND.

SO KESSLER WILL BE BURIED LIKE DI MANNO.

YEAH, LIKE A DOG...

WITHOUT CEREMONY...

60

IN HOLLAND, THINGS ONCE AGAIN BEGAN DEVELOPING TOO FAST FOR OUR TIRED MINDS, ALREADY WORN BY THE PACES WE'D PUT THEM THROUGH. IT TOOK US ONLY ONE NIGHT IN AMSTERDAM TO DISCOVER THAT KESSLER HAD DIED FOR NOTHING.

WE SHOULD GET SOMETHING TO EAT, ANYWAY.

YOU THINK SO?

BECAUSE THE ORDER WAS WELL AND TRULY THERE, EVEN IF WE DIDN'T KNOW WHERE EXACTLY IT WAS.

DAAR KOMEN DE SAUCIJSJES!

STRANGE CROWD GATHERING OUTSIDE...

LET'S GO FIND OUT.

WHAT'S HAPPENING?

AN ATTACK...

SOME EXPLOSIONS! THEY'RE SAYING DOZENS ARE DEAD.

THE POLICE AREN'T EVEN THERE YET.

LUCKILY THE RADIO WAS THERE TO COVER THE FESTIVAL, OTHERWISE...

DE VERWARRING IS ALGEHEEL...

BUT WHAT ARE THEY SAYING?!

HANG ON! THEY'VE JUST RECEIVED A STATEMENT...

...SIGNED BY THE BLACK ORDER BRIGADE...

SAINTS ALIVE...

BUT WE LOOK LIKE FOOLS! FOOLS FOR ARRIVING TOO LATE AGAIN!!!

YOU SHOULD BE ASHAMED TO WORRY ABOUT WHAT WE LOOK LIKE DURING SUCH A TRAGEDY, CASTEJON.

61

DE TERRORISTEN HEBBEN EEN VOORBEELD WILLEN STELLEN...

THEY DID IT TO MAKE AN EXAMPLE... THE STATEMENT MENTIONS DECADENT MUSIC... IT'S A MESSAGE THAT EUROPE IS DEGENERATING.

MADRE DE DIOS! WHAT ON EARTH ARE WE DOING HERE, SO USELESSLY!

WAIT. THERE IS A WAY WE COULD MAKE OURSELVES USEFUL.

WE NEED VOLUNTEERS TO HELP THE INJURED! ARE YOU WITH US?

HELL YES!!!

HEY, YOU OLD MEN LOOK LIKE YOU COULD USE A BIT OF HELP YOURSELVES!

SEEMS LIKE THIS LITTLE IDIOT IS ASKING FOR MY FIST IN HIS FACE!

STOP IT, CASTEJON. HE MUST TAKE US FOR TOURISTS, AND THAT'S JUST FINE WITH US.

THEN GET ABOARD! WE'RE LEAVING.

WATCH OUT, I'M JUMPING!

OWW!

VRIJDAG

ONLY CONFUSED MEMORIES REMAIN OF THAT HORRIBLE NIGHT.

VRIJDAG

62

BOATS MOVING TO AND FRO IN THE DARK AND MISTY SUMMER NIGHT...

MUTILATED CORPSES AND THE WAILING WOUNDED BEING CARRIED THROUGH THE CONFUSION...

SPOTLIGHTS SLICING THROUGH TREES WITH RUSTLING LEAVES...

AND ABOVE ALL, AN IMPRESSION OF CONSTANT, CONSTANT VIOLENCE.

MAKE WAY! MAKE WAY!!

LET ME THROUGH, FOR PITY'S SAKE !!!

YOU BASTARDS, HIS KID IS DYING!

MIND YOUR OWN BUSINESS, ASSHOLE!

AND PERHAPS EVEN AN IMPRESSION OF ABSURDITY...

I DON'T GET IT, MAN, DID WE TAKE TOO BIG A DOSE...?

ME, I JUST HAD A LITTLE JOINT.

NO MORE MUSIC?

GO TO SLEEP, JOOP, IT'S JUST A BAD TRIP.

YES, BITTER ABSURDITY.

LOOKS LIKE TWO GUYS FROM THE BLACK ORDER WERE KILLED ON THE SPOT!

ONE OF THE DEVICES WAS BADLY PLACED.

WHERE ?

THERE...

65

VERY BITTER...

GOOD GOD, HANS HEINKEL, FROM THE CONDOR LEGION!

YEAH, HEINKEL AND PISCIOTTA, MUSSOLINI'S TANK COMMANDER. THEY'VE HARDLY CHANGED.

SAY, DON'T YOU THINK THEY LOOK JUST LIKE US?

OH PLEASE, BARSAC, JUST SHUT UP!

IT'S NOT A PRETTY SIGHT...

WHAT SPOILS IT FOR ME IS THAT WE HAD NOTHING TO DO WITH THEIR DEATHS.

SO MUCH FOR CHRISTIAN CHARITY.

SAY, DON'T YOU THINK PEOPLE ARE STARTING TO LOOK AT US TOO CURIOUSLY?

YOU'RE RIGHT, KATZ! BESIDES HERE COME THE COPS. WE HAVE TO GET OUT OF HERE.

I'D EVEN SAY WE HAVE TO GET OUT OF THE COUNTRY... AND FAST!

WITH ALL THE CONFUSION, THAT SHOULDN'T BE TOO HARD.

AND OUR THINGS?

TOO BAD! WE'VE GOT ALL THE CASH. THAT'S THE MAIN THING.

HEEEY! GET ME OUT OF HERE!!! I'M... GLRBGRL...

CERT TO VEM DO PRDELE!!

CALM DOWN, STRANSKY!

HEY, OVER HERE!

DO YOU SEE WHAT I SEE?

HMM... EXCELLENT IDEA, MY OLD FRIEND.

DESERTED...

EVERYONE MUST BE HELPING THE WOUNDED.

DOES ANYONE KNOW HOW TO MAKE THIS THING GO?

WELL, SINCE I USED TO BE IN THE ROYAL NAVY...

FULL STEAM AHEAD!

FANTASTIC!

LISTEN, AVIDSEN, THIS BARGE MAY NOT BE BRAND-NEW, BUT IT'S WORTH SOMETHING TO THE OWNERS.

VERY TRUE, BARSAC. WITH ALL OUR MONEY, WE CAN AFFORD TO LEAVE THEM AN ENVELOPE STUFFED WITH DEUTSCHE MARKS.

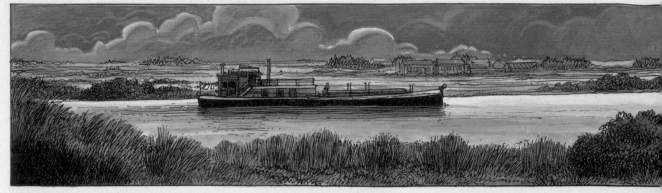

WHERE'RE WE HEADED?

DON'T KNOW...

HEY, I FOUND SOME RIVER MAPS.

THAT'S A START.

AND I JUST HEARD SOMETHING ON THE RADIO.

WELL?

IT SEEMS THE BRIGADE HAS LEFT ITS LAIR, A SMALL CARGO BOAT ALONG THE NOORDOOST POLDER. THEY MENTIONED A HELICOPTER HEADING TOWARDS THE SOUTH.

SO WE GO SOUTH!

WELL, IT'S NOT AS IF WE CAN TAKE THE BOAT TO THE NORTH SEA, ANYWAY.

AHEM... THERE'S ONE MORE THING... KESSLER AND THE GIRL HAVE BEEN FOUND ....

...AND INTERPOL HAS ISSUED A WARRANT FOR OUR ARREST.

WELL AT LEAST THEY'VE STOPPED CONFUSING US WITH THOSE OTHER BASTARDS.

SOME COMFORT ...

NOT TO MENTION THAT IT WON'T MAKE OUR TRIP ANY EASIER.

NOT THE WAY THINGS ARE.

66

IN FACT, THE LOW JOURNEY SOUTH WENT WITHOUT A HITCH. IT SEEMED THAT AVIDSEN'S STASH WAS INEXHAUSTIBLE.

WILLMA

IT ALLOWED US TO RE-PAINT THE BARGE AND A LOT OF OTHER THINGS BESIDES. PERHAPS WE WERE EVEN STARTING TO BECOME GOOD SAILORS.

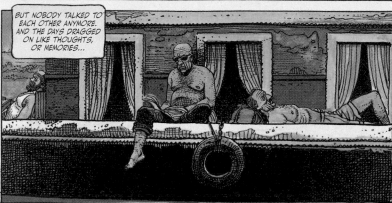

BUT NOBODY TALKED TO EACH OTHER ANYMORE. AND THE DAYS DRAGGED ON LIKE THOUGHTS, OR MEMORIES...

MEMORIES OF THE DEAD...DONAHUE... TADELL...DI MANNO... KESSLER...LOTTE... AND ALL THOSE YOUNG PEOPLE IN A PEACEFUL PASTURE MEANT FOR COWS.

WANDERING THOUGHTS, AMONG WHICH WERE MIXED A THIRST FOR VENGEANCE, THE DESIRE TO FORGET, A TASTE FOR OBLIVION, AND RHEUMATISM, PERHAPS AGGRAVATED BY THE HUMIDITY. MORE THAN EVER, EVERYTHING WAS A BLUR.

I'LL MAKE THE CALL, JUST IN CASE...

OUR ARRIVAL IN PARIS WAS MADE QUIETLY. AUTUMN HAD BEGUN TO COLOR THE TREES ON THE ILE DE LA GRANDE JATTE. LEAVES WERE CLINGING TO MOORINGS ON THE JETTY.

67

THAT SAME EVENING, IN A BISTRO ON THE MONTROUGE, AN OLD ANARCHIST FRIEND, WHO HAD BEEN IN THE BRIGADES HIMSELF, WAS WAITING FOR US, DRINKING A SUZE...

BUVEZ CHOKY

HE WASN'T ALONE.

YOU!?

GOOD GOD!!! WE HAD JUST ABOUT FORGOTTEN YOU!

DON'T WORRY...I'M USED TO IT.

AT LEAST YOU GOT OUT! THAT'S MORE THAN MOST OF US, YOU KNOW.

YEAH...WITH A FRACTURED COLLARBONE THAT TOOK SIX MONTHS TO HEAL.

AND DONAHUE?

DONAHUE? UNDER TEN FEET OF SNOW IN WINTER... LESS, IN SUMMER.

AND WHAT ARE YOU DOING HERE?

OH, ANDRÉ AND I KNOW EACH OTHER PRETTY WELL.

HE KNOWS SOMETHING ABOUT THE MEN YOU'RE LOOKING FOR.

SERVICE NON COMPRIS

BOISSONS

THEY'RE IN FRANCE, RIGHT?

YES, I FOUND OUT FROM AN OLD ARAB FRIEND...A STROKE OF LUCK...

A STROKE OF LUCK? WELL, THAT WOULD BE THE FIRST ONE WE'VE HAD SINCE PRITCH PHONED US TO WIPE OUT THOSE BASTARDS!

WC

RUE DE BAGNEUX

L D'OR

AMOS BIÈRE DE METZ

S

IF THAT'S STILL WHAT YOU WANT TO DO, I THINK THERE'S A GOOD CHANCE.

WE'RE LISTENING...

BIÈRE SUPÉRIEURE BOCK

BUVEZ CHOKY

DEHORS GINOUX!

68

TWO WEEKS LATER, IT WAS TIME FOR SOME BICYCLE TOURING. BUT NOW THE WARM DAYS WERE FAR BEHIND US, AND THE WIND BLEW VIOLENTLY ACROSS THE MILLEVACHES PLATEAU.

MY...HUFF...ACHING KNEES...

CAN YOU...HUFF...SEE THE TOP?

WE'RE NEVER GOING TO GET THERE.

JUST KEEP GOING!

WITH ALL THE EQUIPMENT LOADED INTO BAGS ON THE BICYCLES, THE DRIZZLE-SWEPT MOUNTAIN WAS A TOUGH RIDE, EVEN ON THE WAY DOWN.

WE *DEFINITELY* COULD HAVE MADE OTHER ARRANGEMENTS.

THIS ISN'T THE TIME TO DISCUSS IT!

YOU ALL KNOW VERY WELL THERE'S NO OTHER WAY TO APPROACH THEIR HIDEOUT WITHOUT AROUSING SUSPICION.

IT'S TIME TO GO DOWN.

LISTEN, BARSAC, I WANTED TO TELL YOU...

THERE IT IS! AN OLD FARMHOUSE REFITTED WITH MODERN COMFORTS. THEY HAVE EVERYTHING THEY NEED...FIRING RANGES...ALL KINDS OF WEAPONS...AND GUARDS PATROLLING DAY AND NIGHT.

YEAH?

WE UNDERSTAND YOUR CONVICTIONS...

BAH, THERE'S NOTHING WORSE THAN LAYMEN MORALIZING. HIJO DE PUTA, *LET'S GO!*

69

IF YOU DON'T WANT TO COME, MY FRIEND, YOU'RE FREE NOT TO.

I COMMITTED MYSELF, AND I HAVE RESPECT FOR THE DEAD. I'LL COME DOWN, BUT I WON'T FIGHT.

SETTLE DOWN, COMRADES! AND RATHER LET US BEGIN BY CELEBRATING THE MOMENT WE'VE AWAITED FOR SO LONG!

YEAH, MAYBE YOU'RE RIGHT.

SUICIDE IS A MORTAL SIN, COMMANDER BARSAC!

LOOK, CASTEJON, YOU'RE STARTING TO GET ON OUR NERVES!!! YOU DIDN'T JOIN OUR CRUSADE TO PREACH...*SO SHUT IT!!!*

WE CAN CELEBRATE HERE. THE RAIN HAS STOPPED.

IN ANY CASE WE CAN'T TAKE THE BICYCLES ANY FARTHER.

COME ON, LET'S GET OUT THE BOTTLES!

DAMN!

HE SAID BOTTLES, NOT GUNS!

AND WHAT SHOULD WE DRINK TO? TO THE PAST? TO THE FUTURE?

TO THE *PRESENT,* WHICH IS ALL WE HAVE LEFT!

PLOP

TO THE PRESENT!!!

HERE, PASS ME THE FOIE GRAS.

HEADS UP!

THIS IS IT, HERE THEY COME.

WHAT ARE YOU DOING HERE?

JUST WHAT IT LOOKS LIKE... HAVING A PICNIC!

DIDN'T YOU KNOW THIS IS PRIVATE PROPERTY?

UM, NO.

YOU'RE GOING TO HAVE TO CLEAR OFF IMMEDIATELY!

HEY, LISTEN... IT'S JUST A VETERANS' RALLY.

WE ALL USED TO BE COMPETITORS IN THE TOUR DE FRANCE.

OH YEAH? THAT'S INTERESTING, BECAUSE MY BROTHER-IN-LAW USED TO...

WELL DON'T STAND HERE CHATTING WITH THESE OLD FOOLS, JOE!

FINE, FINISH YOUR GRUB AND THEN BE OUT OF HERE BY NIGHTFALL. OKAY? OTHERWISE, VETERANS OR NOT, WE'LL MAKE YOU EAT YOUR HANDLEBARS.

THANK YOU, GENTLEMEN, THANK YOU!

I SWEAR, BETWEEN THESE GUYS AND THE OLD DROOLERS DOWN BELOW, THERE'S HARDLY ANY ROOM FOR US YOUNG ONES!

THAT'S GERONTOCRACY FOR YOU!

HEY MAN, JUST BECAUSE YOU WENT TO COLLEGE DOESN'T MEAN YOU HAVE TO GET ALL UPPITY WITH ME.

NO USE GETTING WORKED UP, JOE! JUST HEAD UP TO THE LOOKOUT POST AND MAKE SURE THEY ACTUALLY LEAVE.

THAT WORKED PERFECTLY!

YEAH, NOW WE CAN MOVE ON TO THE NEXT PHASE.

IN A QUARTER OF AN HOUR IT WILL BE DARK.

ARE ALL OF YOU CLEAR ABOUT THE PLAN?

VERY CLEAR, MY FRIEND.

OKAY. I'LL TAKE CARE OF MAKING THEM THINK YOU'VE GONE.

THOSE PORTABLE LIGHTS SHOULD FOOL THEM.

DONE.

WHAT ARE WE WAITING FOR?

NOTHING, LET'S GO!

HOW TO RECOUNT THE THINGS THAT NEXT CAME TO PASS IN THAT PLACE ALREADY ENCRUSTED WITH THE COLD OF THE COMING WINTER?

THE DRUNKEN GUARD WAS NEUTRALIZED AS PLANNED, AND HIS TWO DOGS BARELY HAD TIME TO BARK.

WE HAD ALSO ANTICIPATED THE FIRST SOUNDING OF THE ALARM, WHICH REMAINED WITHOUT CONSEQUENCE.

WHAZZAT?

AH, MUST BE JUST JOSEPH BEATING HIS HOUNDS!

BY THE WAY, I JUST SAW THOSE OLD GUYS GET ON THEIR WAY AGAIN.

A FEW MINUTES LATER, THE MACHINE GUN WAS LINED UP WITH THE MAIN DOOR.

PASS ME THAT CLIP!

THE ONLY THING LEFT WAS TO QUIETLY SET THE PLASTIC EXPLOSIVE CHARGES. EVERYTHING SEEMED TO PROGRESS AS SMOOTHLY AND AS INEVITABLY AS A NIGHTMARE, WITH ITS HORRIBLE LOGIC.

IT WAS A STRANGE FEELING, FINALLY SEEING THE MEN WE HAD FOLLOWED FOR SO LONG, SO CLOSE TO US...

...JOAQUIN DE VALLELLANO, THE GUERILLA FROM CHRIST THE KING, HAVING A FOOTBATH...

...DU BUSQUET, A SURVIVOR OF VICHY AND THE OAS, HALF-HEARTEDLY PAWING THE LOCAL HELP...

...JAVIER, ASSASSIN FROM THE LEGION AZUL, QUIETLY READING THE LIVES OF THE SAINTS...

...COLPIN, THE FRENCH MERCENARY, PLAYING DARTS WITH HIS ITALIAN FRIEND IN A ROOMFUL OF MEN DRINKING BEER.

CONTEMPTIBLE OLD MEN, BEING WATCHED BY OTHER OLD MEN, PERHAPS JUST AS CONTEMPTIBLE.

WITHOUT A DOUBT, HELL IS WHAT THEY DESERVED, AND WITHOUT A DOUBT, WE DESERVED IT AS MUCH AS THEY DID.

BECAUSE HELL IS WHAT IT WAS!

LET'S GO, BROTHERS !!!

HELL FOR JOAQUIN DE VALLELLANO...

HA HA HA!

FOR FELIPE CASTEJON...

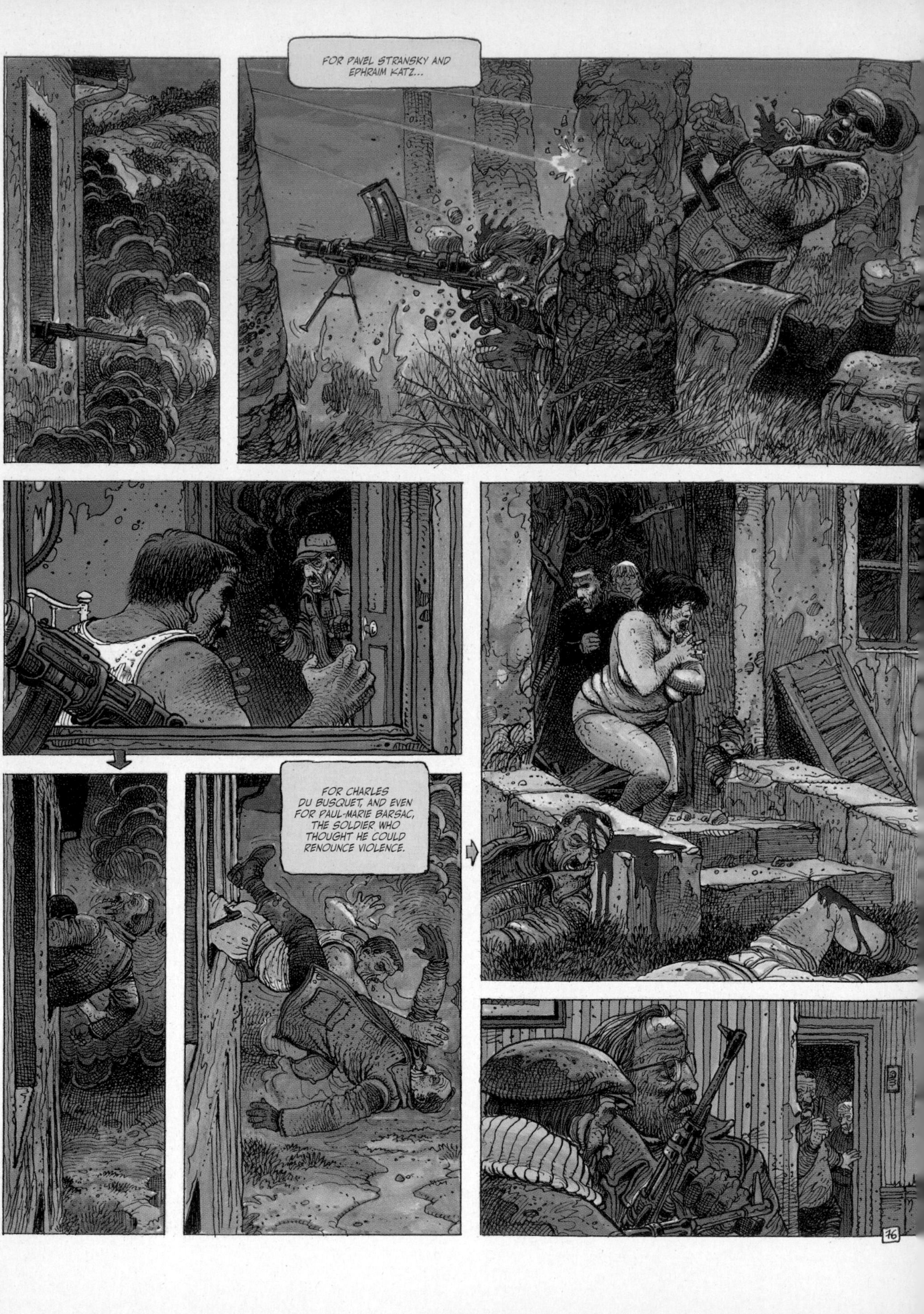
FOR PAVEL STRANSKY AND EPHRAIM KATZ...
FOR CHARLES DU BUSQUET, AND EVEN FOR PAUL-MARIE BARSAC, THE SOLDIER WHO THOUGHT HE COULD RENOUNCE VIOLENCE.
16

ELL FOR
ALFRED
OLPIN AND
ANCISCO
AVIER...

AND FINALLY, HELL FOR CHRISTIAN AVIDSEN.

GET IN! WITH THE ARMS THEY'VE GOT STORED IN THERE, IT'S ALL GOING TO BLOW!

AND WHAT DO YOU THINK YOU'RE DOING HERE?

OH, I JUST HADN'T LEFT YET, THAT'S ALL.

PENG

AAH!

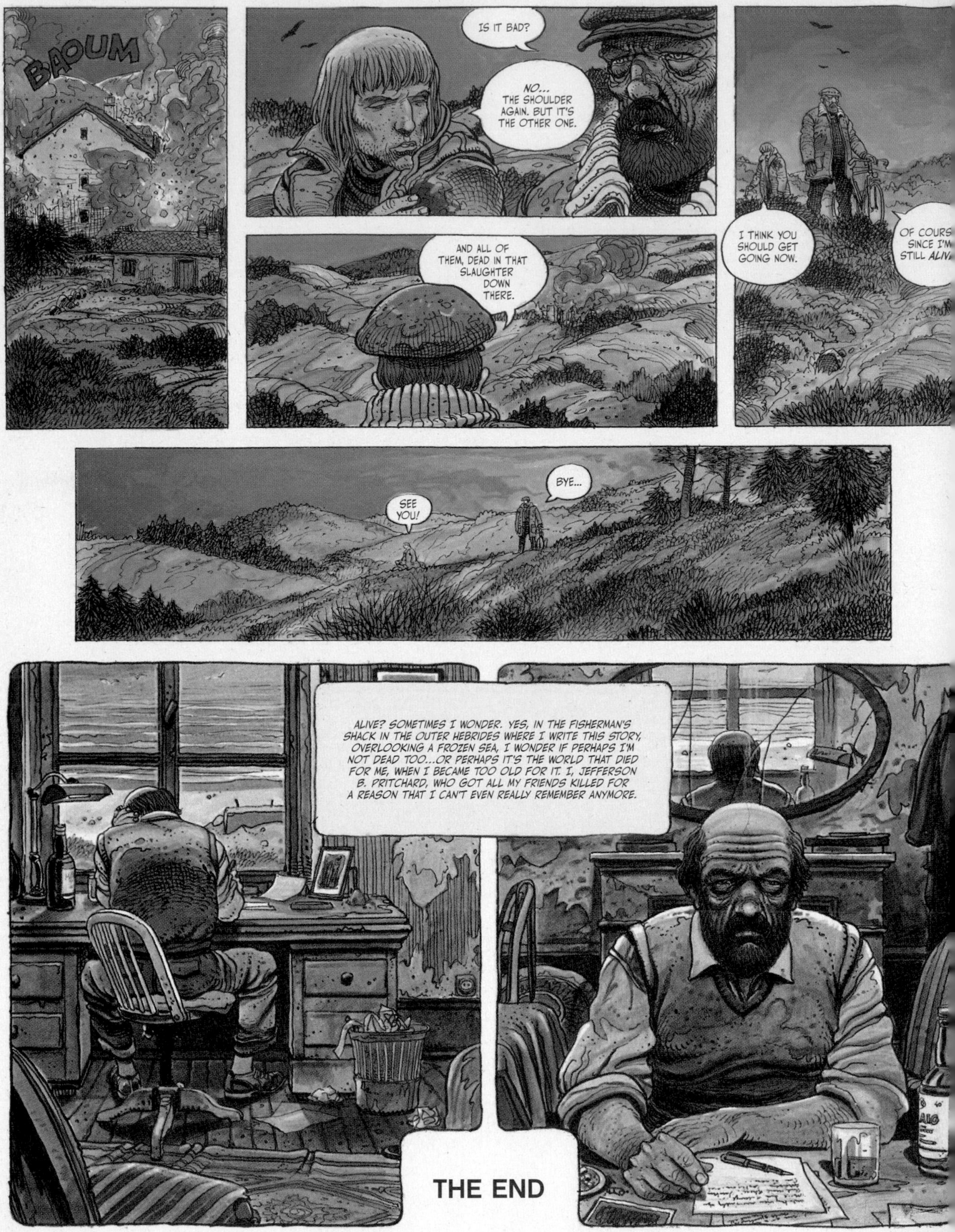
BAOUM
IS IT BAD?
NO... THE SHOULDER AGAIN. BUT IT'S THE OTHER ONE.
AND ALL OF THEM, DEAD IN THAT SLAUGHTER DOWN THERE.
I THINK YOU SHOULD GET GOING NOW.
SEE YOU!
BYE...
ALIVE? SOMETIMES I WONDER. YES, IN THE FISHERMAN'S SHACK IN THE OUTER HEBRIDES WHERE I WRITE THIS STORY, OVERLOOKING A FROZEN SEA, I WONDER IF PERHAPS I'M NOT DEAD TOO...OR PERHAPS IT'S THE WORLD THAT DIED FOR ME, WHEN I BECAME TOO OLD FOR IT. I, JEFFERSON B. PRITCHARD, WHO GOT ALL MY FRIENDS KILLED FOR A REASON THAT I CAN'T EVEN REALLY REMEMBER ANYMORE.
THE END

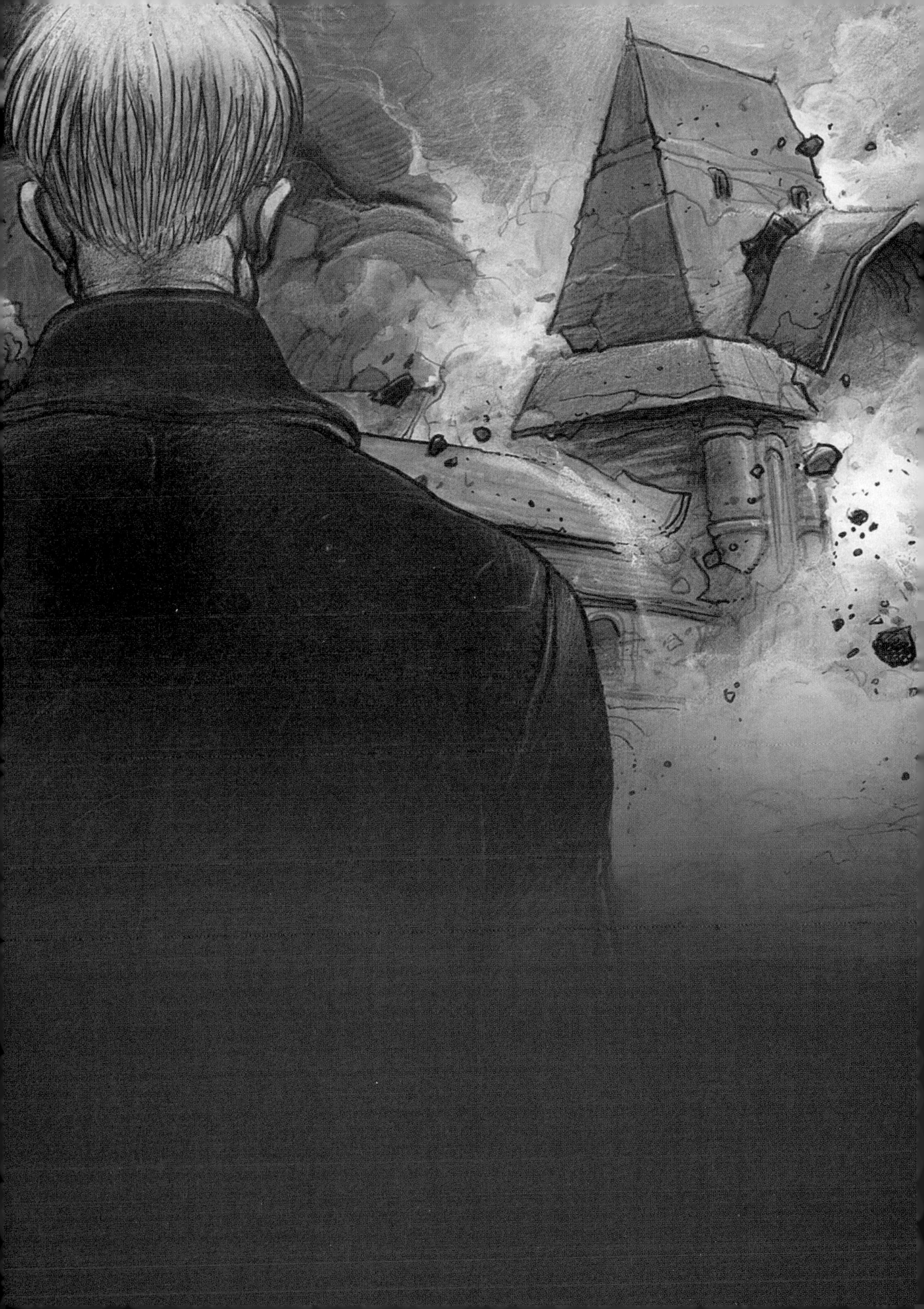

"You've acquired a taste for power, like the taste for rare meat."
—GYÖRGY KONRAD

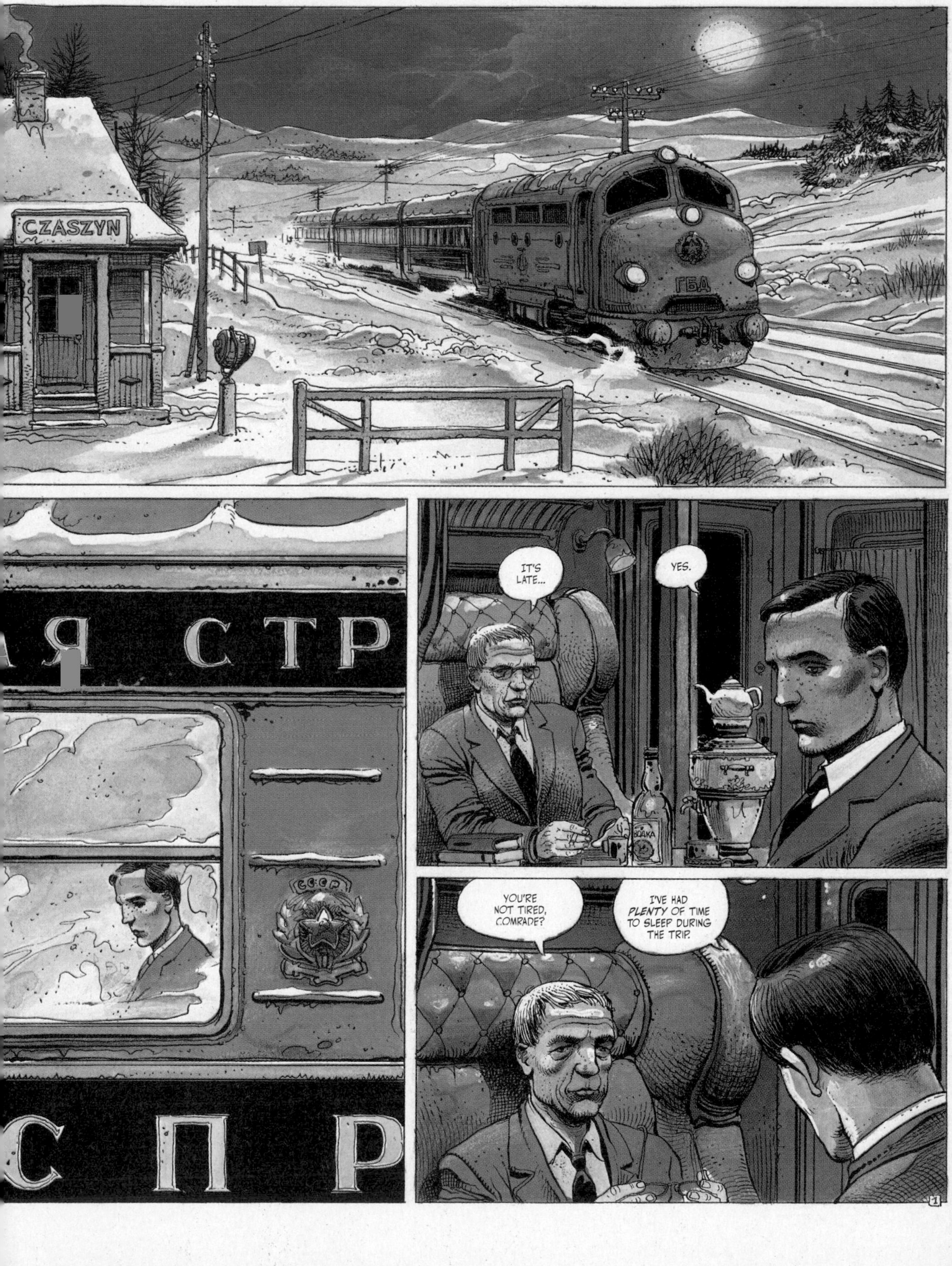
CZASZYN
ГБД
Я СТР
С П Р
IT'S LATE...
YES.
YOU'RE NOT TIRED, COMRADE?
I'VE HAD *PLENTY* OF TIME TO SLEEP DURING THE TRIP.

AND *HIM?* DO YOU THINK HE'S ASLEEP?

MAYBE...

THAT WILL CALL FOR SOME MORE VODKA!

I'LL BE BETTER OFF WITH TEA, I THINK....

YOU'RE NOT *SERIOUS?*

DRRRR

MAYBE NOT. HE *HARDLY* SLEEPS ANYMORE.

TELL ME ABOUT HIM.

⑩

YOU REMIND ME VERY MUCH OF MY EARLY DAYS, AS I WAS COMPLETING MY STUDIES AT MOSCOW UNIVERSITY.

WHY'S THAT?

LIKE YOU, I WANTED TO UNDERSTAND THINGS AS THEY REALLY HAPPENED, BUT WITH US, AS YOU KNOW, HISTORY CAN BE *MUTABLE.*

WELL, YES, BUT...

ПРИНЕСИ НАМ ЕЩЁ ВОДКИ!

СЕЙЧАС!

ПОЖАЛУЙСТА...

TRUE. IT SHOULDN'T REALLY BE SAID THAT WAY. STILL, THERE ARE *MANY* WAYS TO RECOUNT THE LONG LIFE OF A REVOLUTIONARY HERO.

⑲

YOU SEE, VASSILY ALEXANDROVICH CHEVCHENKO'S LIFE INVOLVES SO MANY CONFLICTING ELEMENTS.

SOME ELEMENTS PRESENT HIM IN THE EXALTED LIGHT OF SOCIALISM IN THE MAKING.

"THE ENCOUNTER OF YOUNG VASSILY ALEXANDROVICH, BARELY 20 YEARS OLD, WITH LENIN AND THE BOLSHEVIKS IN EXILE...

"HIS INVOLVEMENT WITH THE PETROGRAD SOVIET, AND THE SEIZING OF THE WINTER PALACE ON AN AUTUMN EVENING IN 1917...

"THE FORMATION OF THE FIRST RED ARMY UNITS, WHICH SPRUNG UP TO FIGHT THE OPPONENTS, BOTH INTERNAL AND EXTERNAL, OF THE REGIME...

"VASSILY ALEXANDROVICH SPOKE TO ME OFTEN OF HIS BRAVEST SOLDIER AT THAT TIME, AN AGELESS MUZHIK NAMED ZHUCHENKO...

"THE STRUGGLE AGAINST FAMINE, WHILE SUPPLY TRAINS WERE BEING ATTACKED AND LOOTED BEFORE EVEN ARRIVING IN THE TOWNS...

"THE CREATION OF A NEW NATION UPON THE RUINS OF THE TSARIST EMPIRE...

"THE INCREDIBLE EFFORTS OF AN ENTIRE COUNTRY PREPARING FOR INDUSTRIALIZATION AND TECHNOLOGICAL ADVANCEMENT...

"THEN, A GOOD DEAL LATER, THE HEROIC BATTLE AGAINST THE NAZI INVADERS.

IT'S *TRUE*, ALL OF IT. AND YES, VASSILY ALEXANDROVICH WAS AT THE FOREFRONT OF IT ALL.

BUT YOU KNOW VERY WELL, MY YOUNG COMRADE, THAT THE SAME THINGS CAN BE PRESENTED IN A *DIFFERENT* LIGHT...

THE CHEKA, THE G.P.U., THE N.K.V.D., THE K.G.B., TO YOU WESTERNERS THESE ARE JUST NAMES OF SECRET POLICE GROUPS, NAMES THAT FASCINATE OR *HORRIFY* YOU.

"BUT FOR THE REVOLUTIONARY SAILORS OF KRONSTADT WHO ROSE UP IN 1921 AGAINST THE NEW REGIME WITH THE TERRIBLE CRY OF 'DEATH TO THE BOLSHEVIKS, LONG LIVE THE SOVIETS!'

"FOR THE INDEPENDENT GEORGIANS AND FOR THE MANY OTHER PEOPLES COMPELLED AND CONSTRAINED TO JOIN THE UNION..."

"...OR FOR THE MUZHIKS, MOWED DOWN AFTER THEY BECAME DESPERATE ARSONISTS IN ORDER TO RESIST COLLECTIVIZATION..."

"FOR THE PURGE VICTIMS, WHO WOULD BE ARRESTED, DEPORTED, SHOT, OR BETTER YET, WHO WOULD 'COMMIT SUICIDE'..."

"FOR THE OLD GUARD REVOLUTIONARIES WHO WERE ASSIGNED ROLES OF TRAITORS DURING THE PUBLIC SHOW TRIALS OF THE 1930s..."

"FOR ALL OF THEM, AND FOR THE COUNTLESS OTHERS WHO DISAPPEARED, FORGOTTEN FOREVER, HISTORY HAS A DIFFERENT COLOR."

AND VASSILY ALEXANDROVICH CONTRIBUTED TO THE PAINTING OF THAT HISTORY, TOO.

YOU USE HARSH WORDS.

PERHAPS YOU'RE *AFRAID* THAT HE'LL HEAR THEM?

DIDN'T YOU TELL ME THAT FRENCH WAS THE ONE FOREIGN LANGUAGE HE ENJOYED?

THAT'S RIGHT, AND HE CERTAINLY UNDERSTANDS US. BUT SOMETIMES ON NIGHTS LIKE THIS WHEN WE DRANK TOGETHER, WE'D SPEAK IN HIS LANGUAGE.

BESIDES, SINCE HE BECAME CONFINED TO SILENCE, HE LIKES TO HEAR ME TALK FOR HIM. I KNOW IT.

AND IN ANY CASE, THOSE ELEMENTS MIGHT NOT BE THE MAIN POINT IN A LIFE LIKE HIS.

WHAT DO YOU MEAN?

THE PARTY'S ONE THING, AND THE LIFE OF A PARTY MAN'S ANOTHER.

90

HOW GREAT WAS THE INFLUENCE OF HIS GRANDFATHER, WHO VASSILY TOLD ME ABOUT SO OFTEN?

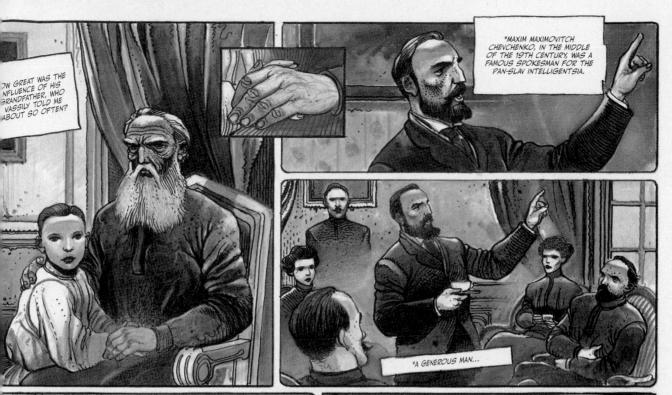

"MAXIM MAXIMOVITCH CHEVCHENKO, IN THE MIDDLE OF THE 19TH CENTURY, WAS A FAMOUS SPOKESMAN FOR THE PAN-SLAV INTELLIGENTSIA.

"A GENEROUS MAN...

"...AND VERY RELIGIOUS, MARKED BY ANTI-WESTERNISM AND FAITH IN THE FUTURE ATTAINMENTS OF MOTHER RUSSIA.

"APPALLED BY THE POVERTY OF THE MASSES, BUT ENDED UP TAKING SANCTUARY MUCH LATER IN A FINE LANDOWNER'S MANSION HE'D COME INTO BY A FAVORABLE MARRIAGE.

"WHICH DIDN'T PREVENT HIM FROM LENDING SUPPORT TO THE RISING SOCIAL DEMOCRACY, OR CONTINUING TO TELL STORIES TO VASSILY ALEXANDROVICH, WHOSE FATHER DISAPPEARED PREMATURELY.

"STRANGE STORIES INDEED, LIKE THE ONE ABOUT OUR DISTANT ANCESTORS WHO APPARENTLY WOULD IMPALE THE WHOLE COURT UPON THE DEATH OF A KING.

"JESTERS, KNIGHTS, AND LADIES, PERISHING IN THEIR NOBLEST FINERY, LIKE PIECES IN A GIGANTIC CHESS GAME.

"A GAME THAT MAXIM MAXIMOVICH TAUGHT HIS GRANDSON IN THE QUIET GARDEN AT HIS DACHA IN THE CRIMEA.

"JUST AS HE TAUGHT HIM TO HUNT HARE AND WOLF ACROSS THE VAST MUDDY PLAINS.

YOU SEE? HUNTING, AND CHESS. VASSILY ALEXANDROVICH'S TWO GREAT PASSIONS, BESIDES POLITICS. ALTHOUGH...

ALTHOUGH WHAT?

ALTHOUGH IT *REALLY* ALL COMES DOWN TO THE SAME THING...POWER.

POWER, WHICH SOMETIMES MEANS CONQUER OR BE CONQUERED, KILL OR BE KILLED.

11

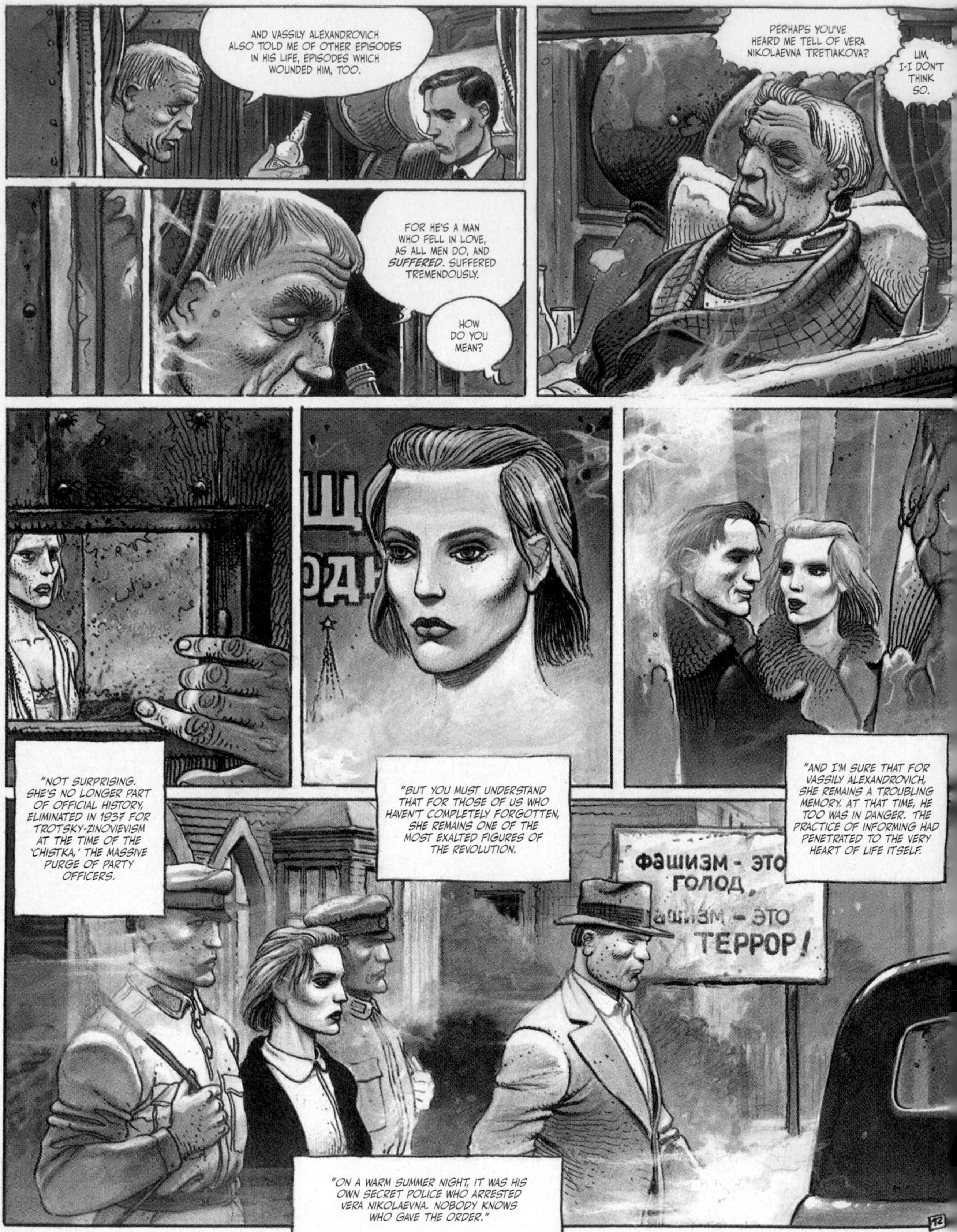

AND VASSILY ALEXANDROVICH ALSO TOLD ME OF OTHER EPISODES IN HIS LIFE, EPISODES WHICH WOUNDED HIM, TOO.
FOR HE'S A MAN WHO FELL IN LOVE, AS ALL MEN DO, AND *SUFFERED*. SUFFERED TREMENDOUSLY.
HOW DO YOU MEAN?
PERHAPS YOU'VE HEARD ME TELL OF VERA NIKOLAEVNA TRETIAKOVA?
UM, I-I DON'T THINK SO.
"NOT SURPRISING. SHE'S NO LONGER PART OF OFFICIAL HISTORY, ELIMINATED IN 1937 FOR TROTSKY-ZINOVIEVISM AT THE TIME OF THE 'CHISTKA,' THE MASSIVE PURGE OF PARTY OFFICERS.
"BUT YOU MUST UNDERSTAND THAT FOR THOSE OF US WHO HAVEN'T COMPLETELY FORGOTTEN, SHE REMAINS ONE OF THE MOST EXALTED FIGURES OF THE REVOLUTION.
"AND I'M SURE THAT FOR VASSILY ALEXANDROVICH, SHE REMAINS A TROUBLING MEMORY. AT THAT TIME, HE TOO WAS IN DANGER. THE PRACTICE OF INFORMING HAD PENETRATED TO THE VERY HEART OF LIFE ITSELF.
ФАШИЗМ - ЭТО ГОЛОД, ФАШИЗМ - ЭТО ТЕРРОР!
"ON A WARM SUMMER NIGHT, IT WAS HIS OWN SECRET POLICE WHO ARRESTED VERA NIKOLAEVNA. NOBODY KNOWS WHO GAVE THE ORDER."
12

AND THEN WHAT?

SHE DIED.

AND THEN WHAT?

HMPH...

I DIDN'T MEET GENERAL CHEVCHENKO UNTIL MUCH LATER, AFTER WORLD WAR II, IN WHICH I HAD SERVED UNDER HIM.

"HE HONORED ME, EVGENY GOLOZOV, BY TAKING ME ON AS HIS INTERPRETER, SECRETARY, AND CONFIDANT.

"IT WAS THE ERA OF THE CREATION OF THE COMINFORM, AND STALIN REIGNED AS ABSOLUTE MASTER OVER THE SOVIET NATIONS.

СПАСИБО РОДНОМУ СТАЛИНУ

ЛЮ

"HE AND I OFTEN TRAVELED TO THE PLACES CONNECTED BY THE TRAIN WE'RE RIDING FROM MOSCOW.

"ONCE AGAIN THERE WERE PURGES, THIS TIME IN HUNGARY, BULGARIA, POLAND, CZECHOSLOVAKIA.

VASSILY ALEXANDROVICH BELIEVED THEY WERE *NECESSARY*, AS DID I. AS DID MANY OTHERS, IT SEEMS.

AND NOW?

I DON'T KNOW WHAT HE BELIEVES ANYMORE. HIS LIPS ARE SEALED SINCE THE FACIAL PARALYSIS, AND HIS EXPRESSION *NEVER* CHANGES.

BUT HIS FACULTIES ARE ALL *INTACT*, AREN'T THEY?

COMPLETELY. AS IS MOST OF HIS POWER, ALTHOUGH NOW HE'S JUST AN ORDINARY MEMBER OF THE PRESIDIUM, AND A FEW OTHER PRESTIGIOUS INSTITUTIONS.

AND YOU? WHAT DO YOU BELIEVE?

ME? OH, I'M JUST A HUMBLE POLYGLOT, MUCH LIKE YOURSELF. SO I LISTEN, AND SOMETIMES I DREAM...

LOOK, IT'S DAWN ALREADY.

ARE WE ALMOST THERE?

YES.

THERE'S ONE MORE QUESTION I WANTED TO ASK.

GO AHEAD.

ME...? WHY WAS I CHOSEN FOR THIS TRIP?

I SUPPOSE BECAUSE I WON'T BE HERE FOREVER, AND BECAUSE YOU'RE A GOOD STUDENT WHO KNOWS ALL THE LANGUAGES WE'LL NEED WHEN WE ARRIVE.

OR ELSE IT'S ONE OF THOSE BUREAUCRATIC FLUKES SO COMMON TO OUR SCIENTIFICALLY ORGANIZED REGIME. WHO KNOWS?

OH...

AND NOW LET'S GET SOME REST. I FEAR THE DAYS AHEAD OF US WILL BE BUSY ONES.

I'VE NEVER BEEN ON A HUNT BEFORE.

I WASN'T REFERRING TO THAT, COMRADE.

OH...

97

IT LOOKS LIKE WE'RE ARRIVING.

LET ME HELP YOU FOR ONCE, VASSILY ALEXANDROVICH. THE TRAIN'S PULLING IN TO THE STATION...

KROLÓWKA

WELCOME, VASSILY ALEXANDROVICH, TO THIS HUNT PLANNED *FOR* YOU AND *BY* YOU!

WHO'S THAT?

TADEUSZ BOCZEK. ONE OF OUR OLD FRIENDS FROM POLAND.

DOES HE SPEAK FRENCH TOO?

ALMOST ALL THE GUESTS AT THE HUNT HAVE FRENCH, AS THEIR ONLY LANGUAGE IN COMMON.

YOU WON'T BE OVERWORKED, MY YOUNG COMRADE. UNLESS THEY GET ANGRY, BECAUSE THEN THEY PRETEND THEY CAN'T UNDERSTAND ONE ANOTHER AND CALL ON US.

I SEE.

BAGAZE DO SAMOCHODU!!!

HEY, OLD COMRADE!

GREAT TO SEE YOU AGAIN, EVGENY!

WHERE ARE THE OTHERS?

ACCORDING TO THEORY, TWO OF THEM SHOULD BE ON THIS TRAIN COMING IN NOW.

IN ANY CASE, IT PROVES THAT OUR SOCIALIST TRAINS CAN SOMETIMES RUN ON TIME.

THERE THEY ARE!

THE ONE IN FRONT'S ION NICOLESCU, MEMBER OF THE ROMANIAN CENTRAL COMMITTEE AND HEAD OF THE PARTY POLICE.

THE OTHER ONE, BEHIND HIM, IS JANOS MOLNAR, VICE-MINISTER OF THE INTERIOR IN BUDAPEST.

TO THE CARS, MY FRIENDS! COMRADE VASSILY ALEXANDROVICH IS WAITING FOR US.

HOW HAVE YOU BEEN SINCE WE LAST MET? LET'S SEE...THE HUNT IN THE CARPATHIANS, WASN'T IT?

THAT'S RIGHT.

WHAT'S GOING ON OVER THERE?!

WILL YOU LET GO OF ME!

KIM JEST TEN MEZCZYZYNA? CZEGO ON CHCE?

TO JEST FRANCUZ TWIERDZI ZE GEST TURISTA...WYDAJE NAM SIE, PODEGRZANY.

SUPPOSEDLY A TOURIST. HE CLAIMS TO BE FRENCH.

THE GENERAL DOESN'T WANT ANY TOURISTS OR SPIES AROUND HERE.

FRENCH, DID YOU SAY? PERHAPS I SHOULD--

NO, YOU SHOULDN'T DO ANYTHING. YOU'RE A PRIVATE INTERPRETER, NOT A VOLUNTEER GUIDE FOR INTOURIST. COME ON, INTO THE JEEP. WE'RE GOING!

STRZYŻÓW
ZWOLEN

KROLOWKA

HAS THE GENERAL KNOWN HIS HUNTING COMPANIONS FOR A LONG TIME?

BUT OF COURSE. THEY'RE ALL VERY OLD FRIENDS.

AND TADEUSZ?

A CONSTANT JOKESTER, YOU'LL SEE. SOMETIMES A BIT ECCENTRIC SINCE HE RETIRED TO THIS ESTATE, BUT HIS WIT IS UNPARALLELED.

YES, BUT WHAT WAS HE BEFORE THAT? HIS NAME SOUNDS *FAMILIAR.*

THAT'S ENTIRELY POSSIBLE. HE PLAYED AN IMPORTANT ROLE IN POST-WAR WARSAW.

AND...UM... HE'S JEWISH, ISN'T HE?

CORRECT. *UNFORTUNATELY* FOR HIM, I'M AFRAID. HE SUFFERED A LOT OF VERY NASTY THINGS IN 1967, AND POLAND LOST ONE OF ITS FINEST STATESMEN.

BUT THE ESTATE YOU SEE BEFORE YOU CERTAINLY GAINED ITS FINEST CARETAKER.

I SEE.

POLOWANIE ZABRONIONE WSTĘP WZBRONIONY

DON'T WORRY. YOU'LL HEAR A LOT MORE ABOUT IT, AND VERY SOON. COMRADE TADEUSZ HAS BECOME QUITE TALKATIVE SINCE BEING RELIEVED OF POLITICAL DUTIES. ISN'T THAT RIGHT COMRADE?

AND YOU, EVGENY, STILL THE SAME OLD GOSSIP-MONGER, I SEE.

BUT RATHER THAN DEFAMING MY REPUTATION, WHY DON'T YOU GO AND FIND VASIL, WHO'S ARRIVED ALREADY, AND SHOULD BE WAITING SOMEWHERE INSIDE.

THAT WILL GIVE YOUR YOUNG CHARGE THE CHANCE TO KNOW HIS WAY AROUND, WHILE I SHOW THE NEW ARRIVALS TO THEIR ROOMS.

WHATEVER YOU SAY, MR. CARETAKER.

COME, FOLLOW ME!

THIS PLACE IS FABULOUS!

AH YES, THE DECADENT AND EXPLOITATIVE ARISTOCRACY OF THESE PARTS DIDN'T *NECESSARILY* HAVE BAD TASTE.

AND EVEN IN THE SCIENCES. THAT SHOULD BE THE DOOR TO THE OBSERVATORY.

NOW LET'S SEE, I THINK I'M GETTING AN INKLING OF WHERE WE MIGHT FIND THE GOOD VASIL STROYANOV...

I'LL BET YOU *ANYTHING* YOU LIKE, COMRADE, THAT HE'S ALREADY LEANING ON THE BAR.

THEY TOOK AN INTEREST IN THE ARTS, AS YOU CAN SEE.

WHAT DID I TELL YOU!

AH, SOMEBODY'S HERE AT LAST! I WAS STARTING TO GET BORED!

WELL, YOU WON'T HAVE MUCH CHANCE TO BE BORED DURING OUR NEXT THREE DAYS TOGETHER!

GOOD OLD GOLOZOV! STILL THE SAME, EH?

YOU TOO, BY THE LOOKS OF IT.

WELL, TADEUSZ, WHERE ARE THE OTHERS?

DON'T WORRY, VASIL. THEY'RE COMING.

AH, VASSILY ALEXANDROVICH!!!

THEIR BAGGAGE GOT A BIT SIDETRACKED. THE SERVANTS HERE ARE HARDLY BETTER THAN ANYWHERE ELSE, YOU KNOW.

HMPH...THESE FELLOWS DON'T LIKE US ANY BETTER THAN THEIR FORMER MASTERS.

AND WHY SHOULD THEY? I SUSPECT THEY EVEN FIND US DECIDEDLY LESS REFINED.

STILL IN GREAT SHAPE, EH?

WELL NOW, TADEUSZ, WHAT'S THE PLAN?

TO SHOW YOU SOMETHING THAT SHOULD *AMUSE* YOU. THIS WAY.

I PROPOSE, WHILE WAITING FOR PAVEL TO ARRIVE BY CAR, THAT YOU COME WITH ME TO THE SERVANTS' QUARTERS.

THE SERVANTS' QUARTERS? WHAT FOR?

STRAJK

TO OCCUPY MY SOMEWHAT COMPULSORY LEISURE TIME, I'VE RESTORED THE FALCONRY OF THE VERY HONORED LORD AND SOCIAL PARASITE WHO USED TO INHABIT THE PREMISES.

YOU KNOW I *DON'T* LIKE VIOLENCE.

BUT, I'M SURE YOU'LL AGREE, AN ACT OF VIOLENCE IS ALWAYS BEST THROUGH AN INTERMEDIARY.

TRUE INDEED.

THE TRAINING IS COMPLETE, AND, AS YOU WILL SEE, MY BIRDS ARE IN *TOP* SHAPE.

TO BEGIN WITH, I PRESENT KARL, THE BEST OF MY LONG-WINGED HAWKS.

A SOMEWHAT ARROGANT ANIMAL, BUT *VERY* INTELLIGENT.

BUT WHY "KARL?"

JUST A WHIM, MY GOOD NICOLESCU. A REMINDER OF THE THEORETICAL READINGS OF MY YOUTH, WHEN "DAS KAPITAL" WAS MY BIBLE. YOU'LL UNDERSTAND BETTER WHEN YOU SEE HIM HUNT A CROW FOR PLEASURE.

IT'S *WRONG* TO GIVE OUR FOUNDING FATHER'S NAME TO A BIRD THAT--

RUSZAJ!!

THAT'S MY KARL. HE PREYS SAVAGELY ON BIRDS HE DOESN'T LIKE.

WHAT INTERESTS HIM IS THE BEAUTY OF THE STRIKE, SO TO SPEAK. AND HE TIRES QUICKLY OF THE LIFELESS QUARRY.

YOU'LL SEE MY SPARROW-HAWK IS COMPLETELY *DIFFERENT*.

AN *IGNOBLE* CREATURE, THIS ONE, PERSISTENT AND CRUEL.

HE PREFERS SHADOWY WOODS TO OPEN PLAINS, AND A PLUMP PARTRIDGE TO A GAUNT CROW.

WATCH HIM CLOSELY!

HE'LL STALK HIS VICTIM, THEN PIN IT TO THE GROUND TO TEAR ITS FLESH.

MAGNIFICENT!

YES, WHAT SKILL!

EXCELLENT SHOW! A GOOD IDEA YOU HAD THERE, TADEUSZ.

AND WHAT DO YOU CALL THIS BLOODTHIRSTY SCOUNDREL?

JOSEF. ALSO KNOWN AS "LITTLE FATHER OF THE PEOPLE." HEH HEH...

"OH, VERY FUNNY INDEED. YOU'RE PRACTICING IDEALIST ALLEGORY IN YOUR OLD AGE, TADEUSZ!"

"COME ON, EVGENY, WHERE'S YOUR SENSE OF HUMOR!"

BILAL

24

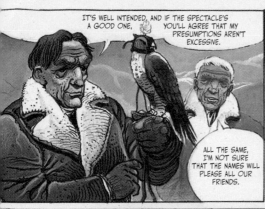

IT'S WELL INTENDED, AND IF THE SPECTACLE'S A GOOD ONE, YOU'LL AGREE THAT MY PRESUMPTIONS AREN'T EXCESSIVE.

ALL THE SAME, I'M NOT SURE THAT THE NAMES WILL PLEASE ALL OUR FRIENDS.

SPEAKING OF OUR FRIENDS, LOOK OVER THERE!

PON

SO, COMRADE, WEREN'T YOU AFRAID TO BRAVE THE SNOW IN THIS ANTIQUE?

PAVEL HAVELKA, COMING DIRECTLY FROM PRAGUE, I IMAGINE...

PAVEL'S IS A STORMY BUT BRILLIANT CAREER.

HE WAS AMONG THOSE WHO TOOK BACK CONTROL OF THE CZECH COMMUNIST PARTY DURING THE "NORMALIZATION" OF 1969.

I SEE...

IT'S READY, SIR.

THIS WAY, FRIENDS! I'VE HAD A SIMPLE BUT SUBSTANTIAL LUNCH PREPARED FOR US. WITH THIS COLD, WE'RE CERTAINLY GOING TO NEED IT.

HEY, YOU THERE! WE'RE MISSING THE MOST IMPORTANT THING! RUN AND FETCH SOME VODKA AND WINE!

YES, VASSILY ALEXANDROVICH, IT'S THE VERY SAME OLD TATRA THAT YOU RODE IN TIME AND TIME AGAIN WITH ME.

"OF COURSE IT ISN'T THE SAME ONE YOU PUT AT MY DISPOSAL WHEN I WAS STILL A SOCIAL DEMOCRAT, BEFORE THE PARTY TOOK POWER IN '48."

COME ON, TELL IT LIKE IT IS, PAVEL! HOW YOU PLAYED WITH SUBMARINES IN THE KREMLIN BEFORE THE PRAGUE COUP, WHICH ENDED UP MAKING A *RESPECTABLE* PARTY-LINE MINISTER OUT OF YOU!

IF YOU LIKE, TADEUSZ, IF YOU LIKE...

BUT I'LL REMIND YOU THAT I DIDN'T RECEIVE ONLY HONOR BY FOLLOWING THE PARTY LINE.

"IN FACT IT WAS IN THE SAME MODEL CAR THAT I WAS ARRESTED FOR BEING AN IMPERIALIST AGENT AND BOURGEOIS NATIONALIST IN '52, DURING THE SLÁNSK TRIAL."

AND THEN WHEN THEY REHABILITATED YOU IN '63?

YES, JANOS, THAT'S *EXACTLY* WHEN I CAME BY THE CAR I HAVE NOW.

VODKA, PLEASE!

"A FOND MEMORY...BUT PERHAPS THE WHOLE ERA CONSTITUTES A FOND MEMORY, ISN'T THAT RIGHT VASSILY ALEXANDROVICH?

"REMEMBER WHEN YOU CAME WITH ME TO THE MINISTRY OF CULTURE TO NEGOTIATE A RECONCILIATION BETWEEN THE INTELLECTUALS AND THE PARTY?

"EXCEPT FOR THAT FOOL VIZEK WHO SPENT ALL HIS TIME ASKING WHO WAS INFILTRATING WHO, THINGS PROGRESSED BEAUTIFULLY.

"BUT I'M SURE YOU ALSO REMEMBER OUR MEETING NEAR THE BORDER, ON AUGUST 15TH, 1968.

"IT WAS ON THE SEAT CUSHIONS OF THIS VERY CAR THAT YOU WARNED ME OF THE RISK OF INVASION BY THE PACT TROOPS.

"I DIDN'T BELIEVE IT ANY MORE THAN DUBCEK DID, AND WE DROVE IN SILENCE FOR A LONG TIME ALONG THE TINY NEARBY MOUNTAIN ROADS.

"BUT ON THE 21ST, I WAS FORCED TO ACCEPT IT, WHEN I ENCOUNTERED RUSSIAN TANKS IN THE STREETS OF MY HOMETOWN."

ЭХ, ИВАН! ВЕРНИСЬ ДОМОЙ!!!

BČEK SVOBODA

USA-VIETNAM USSR-ČSSR

HOJ KAMAREDE! KOHO JSTI VY PRISLI ZABIT? SVOBODU?

ČECH

"AND LIKE THE PRAGUE YOUTHS SAID TO YOUR SOLDIERS, WHAT YOU HAD COME TO CRUSH WAS NOTHING MORE OR LESS THAN FREEDOM. AND YOU WERE THE FIRST ONE TO REALIZE IT."

HAH, I'VE ALWAYS SAID THAT YOUR "SOCIALISM WITH A HUMAN FACE" WAS A GROSS TACTICAL *ERROR.*

NAIVE AND PREMATURE, ANYWAY.

BUT FOR SOMEONE WHO WAS A VICTIM IN AN EARLIER ERA, YOU EMERGED FROM THE TROUBLE *WITHOUT* TOO MUCH FUSS, DIDN'T YOU?

YES, IN A WAY.

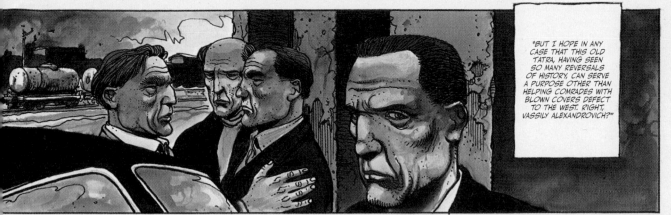

"BUT I HOPE IN ANY CASE THAT THIS OLD TATRA, HAVING SEEN SO MANY REVERSALS OF HISTORY, CAN SERVE A PURPOSE OTHER THAN HELPING COMRADES WITH BLOWN COVERS DEFECT TO THE WEST. RIGHT, VASSILY ALEXANDROVICH?"

AHEM...

YES...

WELL, SHALL WE GO NOW?

ALL RIGHT, FRIENDS! THE DOGS ARE READY!

YOU'RE RIGHT, LET'S NOT WASTE TIME ON IDLE REMINISCENCE. I'LL GO CHANGE.

GET READY, EVERYONE! WE LEAVE IN FIFTEEN MINUTES.

HERE, TAKE THIS.

WHAT, YOU EXPECT ME TO USE ONE OF THOSE?!

YOU'RE SURE GOING TO HAVE TO LEARN TO, KID.

WE'LL HUNT INDIVIDUALLY TO START WITH, LIKE VASSILY ALEXANDROVICH PREFERS. BE VERY SURE TO ALWAYS WALK INTO THE WIND.

INTO THE WIND? BUT I CAN'T EVEN TELL WHICH WAY THE WIND IS COMING FROM, AND--

SILENCE, YOUNG COMRADE! VASSILY ALEXANDROVICH DOESN'T WANT TO HEAR A SINGLE UNNECESSARY WORD WHEN HE'S HUNTING!

MISSED, COMRADE!

114

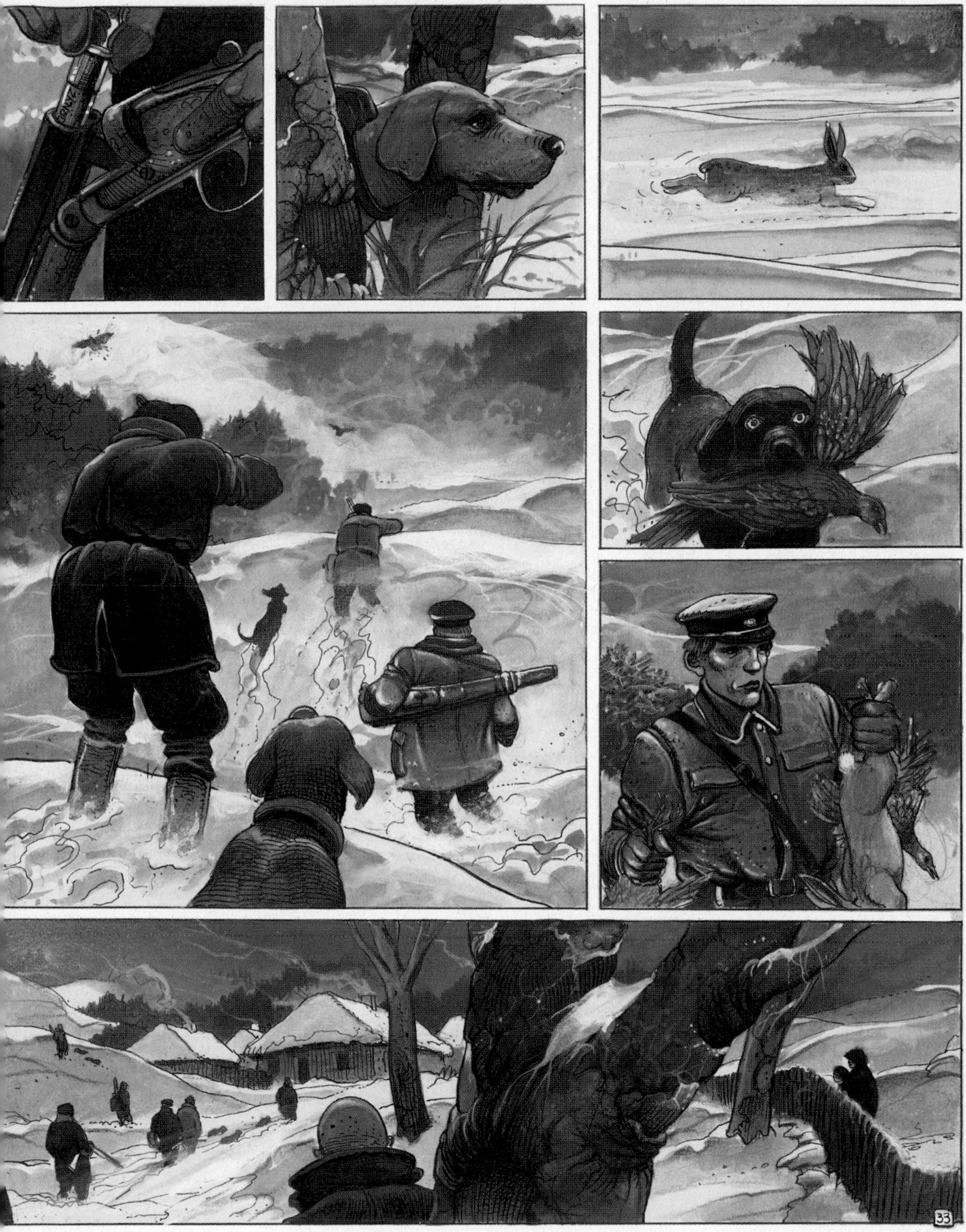
33

DAMN! MISSED!

YOU SEE, MY FRENCH FRIEND, NOT ALL OF THEM ARE CRACK SHOTS.

BUT I CAN TELL THEY'RE ALL BETTER THAN I AM.

IN ANY CASE, THE SUN'S GOING DOWN. IT'S TIME TO HEAD BACK.

34

AN EXCELLENT DAY! THERE'S NO DENYING IT WAS A WELL PLANNED HUNT, TADEUSZ!

LET'S DRINK TO THAT! SOME WHISKY?

YOU KNOW VERY WELL, EVGENY, THAT THE OBJECTS OF TODAY'S SPORTING AFFECTION, YOUR LITTLE FURRED AND FEATHERED FRIENDS, WERE JUST THE BEGINNING.

YOU, VASIL, WOULD DO WELL TO BEWARE THE AFFECTS OF CAPITALIST LIQUOR ON YOUR TONGUE.

HMPH...

DO YOU HEAR THAT? A HELICOPTER.

IT'S THEM! AND RIGHT ON TIME.

THE *REAL* HUNTING BEGINS WHEN OUR LAST GUESTS ARRIVE.

YOU CAN SAY THAT AGAIN! HA, HA HA!

WHERE ARE THEY COMING FROM?

AKADEMGORODOK, WHERE THERE WAS A SUMMIT CONFERENCE ON INDUSTRIAL TRADE BETWEEN UNION-REPUBLICS!!!

BRRR...I'LL NEVER LIKE SIBERIA, UNION-REPUBLICS OR NO UNION-REPUBLICS!

AFTERWARDS THEY TOOK A PLANE TO THE MILITARY AIRSTRIP AT CHERNIGOV, AND THE HELICOPTER BROUGHT THEM HERE.

YOU SEE THAT ONE, WHO LOOKS LIKE ONE OF THE EFFICIENT EXECUTIVES *SO NUMEROUS* IN YOUR PART OF THE WORLD. THAT'S GÜNTHER SCHÜTZ, BORN IN BERLIN AT THE SAME TIME AS NAZISM.

BRILLIANT STUDIES IN PHILOSOPHY, THEN ECONOMY...

SIGNIFICANT THEORETICAL ACTIVITIES, AND INNOVATIVE CONCEPTS IN MATTERS OF PRODUCTION, SO HE WAS *QUICKLY* NOTICED BY VASSILY ALEXANDROVICH WHO APPOINTED HIM A CONSULTANT TO THE EAST GERMAN POLITBURO BEFORE HE DIRECTED THE COMMUNIST PARTY'S UNIVERSITY IN THE G.D.R.

AND NOW?

86

AND NOW, GÜNTHER SCHÜTZ IS ONE OF THE INTELLECTUAL LEADERS OF COMECON. BEFORE HE CAME WE DIDN'T KNOW WHY OUR COMMON MARKET WASN'T WORKING PROPERLY. *NOW, WE KNOW.*

YOU BECOME OBSERVANT, MY FRENCH FRIEND. IN EFFECT, SERGEI SHAVANIDZE IS HIS APPOINTED SUCCESSOR, AND SO ISN'T REQUIRED TO SHOW DEFERENCE TO HIM.

WHAT ABOUT HIM? HE'S NOT GREETING VASSILY ALEXANDROVICH LIKE THE OTHERS.

AND DO YOU THINK IT WORKS BETTER NOW?

NO, BUT KNOWLEDGE ITSELF IS *PRICELESS* IN ANY SCIENTIFIC REGIME SUCH AS OURS.

REALLY NOW...

ANYWAY, YOU GO WITH HIM NOW, INSTEAD OF STANDING HERE CHATTING. HE DOESN'T SPEAK ANY FOREIGN LANGUAGES, IN ADDITION TO WHICH HE DOESN'T LIKE ME AT ALL, SO--

SO YOU'RE GOING TO BE WORKING TOWARDS THE GREATER GOOD OF THE SOCIALIST FACTION, WHOSE FUTURE SERGEI IS IN CHARGE OF LOOKING AFTER.

ВОТ ТВОЙ ПЕРЕВОДНИК, СЕРГЕЙ... ЭТИЙ ФРАНЦУЗ ЕСТЬ СТУДЕНТОМ ПОСЛЕДНЕГО ГОДА МОСКОВСКОГО УНИВЕРСИТЕТА...

ОЧЕНЬ ХОРОШО...

CLEVER, CHOOSING A FRENCHMAN. MORE NEUTRAL THAT WAY.

YES, IT WAS VASSILY ALEXANDROVICH'S IDEA.

НУ, МОЛНАР, КАК ДЕЛА В БУДАПЕШТЕ?

UHH...HOGY VAN BUDAPESTEN?

LET'S NOT WAIT AROUND HERE! INSTEAD WE'LL GO HAVE A DRINK IN THE WINTER GARDEN!

GOOD IDEA!

И В ПРАГЕ, СПОКОЙНО?

AHEM... JESTLI V PRAZE JE KLID?

119

I EVEN SUGGEST THAT WE *INAUGURATE* THE HEATED POOL THAT THEY HAD ME SET UP IN THE BASEMENT.

WHY NOT...? IT WILL RELIEVE THE FATIGUE OF THE HUNT.

AND THE FATIGUE OF TRAVELING, GÜNTHER, WHAT DO YOU SAY?

ELEGANT INSTALLATION.

YES, NOT BAD, THE WHOLE SYSTEM WAS IMPORTED FROM THE UNITED STATES.

I THOUGHT THAT YOUR COUNTRY'S INTERNATIONAL DEFICIT PROHIBITED THAT TYPE OF INDULGENCE.

THAT *DEPENDS* ON WHAT INDULGENCE, AND FOR WHOM, AS YOU EXPERTS KNOW VERY WELL.

I SHOULD REMIND YOU OF MY WRITINGS, TADEUSZ. I *DON'T* APPROVE OF ANY TYPE OF LUXURY SPENDING.

WELL, I ONLY CARRIED OUT THE INSTRUCTIONS OF THE FORMER MANAGEMENT. BESIDES, THEY WON'T BENEFIT FROM IT NOW, SINCE--

YES, THAT'S RIGHT, PRIVILEGE COMES AND GOES. IN THE END, IT'S THE PERMANENT ONES LIKE YOU WHO BENEFIT FROM "LUXURY EXPENSES." RIGHT, GÜNTHER?

HMPH...

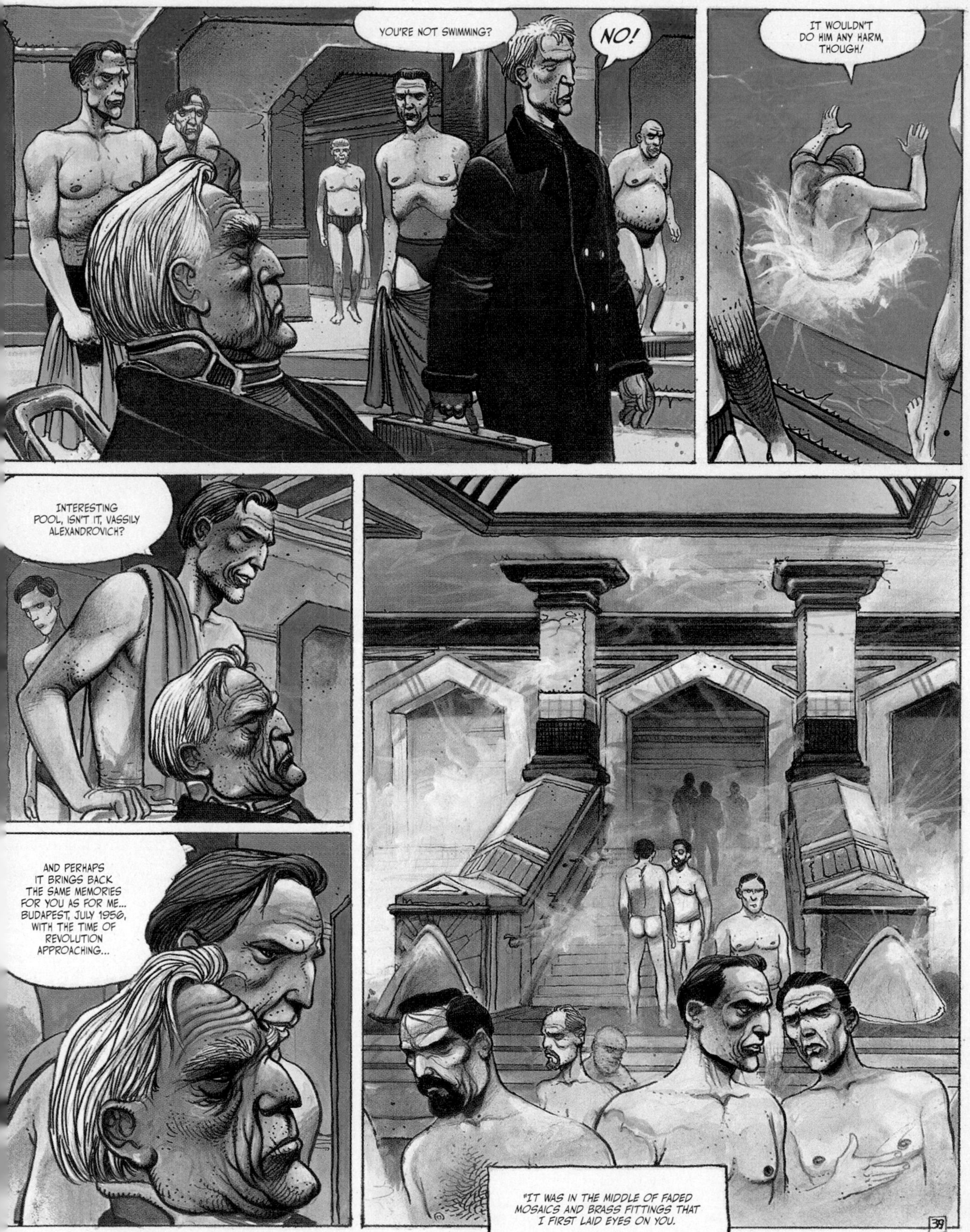
YOU'RE NOT SWIMMING?
NO!
IT WOULDN'T DO HIM ANY HARM, THOUGH!
INTERESTING POOL, ISN'T IT, VASSILY ALEXANDROVICH?
AND PERHAPS IT BRINGS BACK THE SAME MEMORIES FOR YOU AS FOR ME... BUDAPEST, JULY 1956, WITH THE TIME OF REVOLUTION APPROACHING...
"IT WAS IN THE MIDDLE OF FADED MOSAICS AND BRASS FITTINGS THAT I FIRST LAID EYES ON YOU.
39

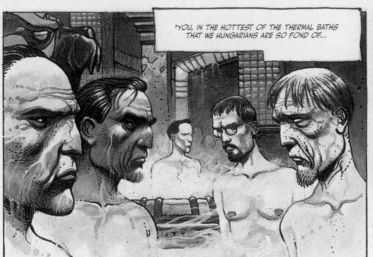

"YOU, IN THE HOTTEST OF THE THERMAL BATHS THAT WE HUNGARIANS ARE SO FOND OF...

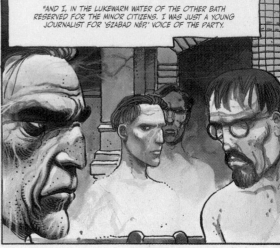

"AND I, IN THE LUKEWARM WATER OF THE OTHER BATH RESERVED FOR THE MINOR CITIZENS. I WAS JUST A YOUNG JOURNALIST FOR 'SZABAD NÉP,' VOICE OF THE PARTY.

"WE COULDN'T MAKE OUT WHAT YOU WERE SAYING. THE RUSH OF WATER SPOUTING FROM THE ANIMAL FOUNTAINS WAS THE ONLY SOUND WE HEARD.

"BUT WE ALL KNEW THAT YOU HAD COME TO DEPOSE THE STALINIST HOLDOUTS WHO HADN'T UNDERSTOOD THAT A CHANGE WAS REQUIRED AFTER KHRUSHCHEV'S RISE TO POWER.

AND BENEATH THE RUSHING FLOW THAT HID HIS FACE, I COULD TELL THAT TIBOR ILLYES WAS *CRYING* AS HE HEARD YOUR DISMISSAL.

40

122

"AN ASTONISHING DISMISSAL INDEED TO AN OLD MILITANT LIKE HIM WHO HAD BEEN ABSOLUTELY DEVOTED TO YOU FOR SO MANY YEARS.

"PRESENTLY EVERYONE MOVED TOWARDS THE HAMMAM, WITH ITS EVEN STEAMIER AND HOTTER ROOMS.

"SILENCE REIGNED, EACH MAN CONTEMPLATING THE OUTCOME YOU WERE TRYING TO PREVENT BY REMODELING AN ADMINISTRATION LOATHED BY THE PEOPLE.

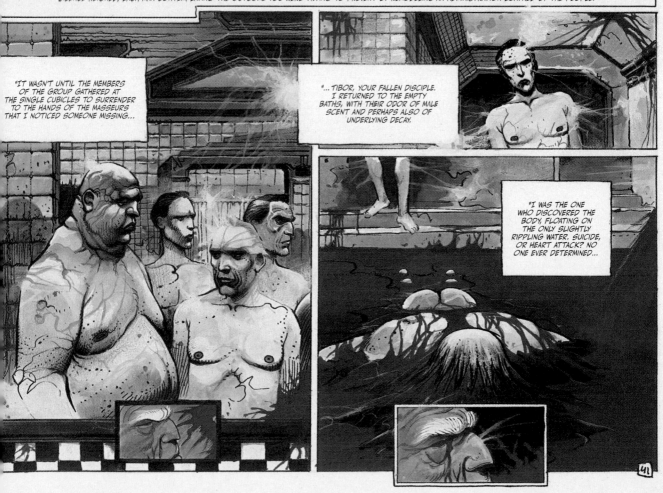

"IT WASN'T UNTIL THE MEMBERS OF THE GROUP GATHERED AT THE SINGLE CUBICLES TO SURRENDER TO THE HANDS OF THE MASSEURS THAT I NOTICED SOMEONE MISSING...

"...TIBOR, YOUR FALLEN DISCIPLE. I RETURNED TO THE EMPTY BATHS, WITH THEIR ODOR OF MALE SCENT AND PERHAPS ALSO OF UNDERLYING DECAY.

"I WAS THE ONE WHO DISCOVERED THE BODY, FLOATING ON THE ONLY SLIGHTLY RIPPLING WATER. SUICIDE, OR HEART ATTACK? NO ONE EVER DETERMINED...

"WAS IT PERHAPS BECAUSE I WAS THE FIRST ONE TO ALERT YOU TO THE INCIDENT THAT YOU STRUCK UP A FRIENDSHIP WITH ME?"

"YES, I OFTEN WONDERED WHY, WHEN YOU RETURNED TO OUR CAPITAL DEVASTATED BY FIGHTING IN THE STREETS, YOU SELECTED ME FROM AMONG MANY OTHERS."

"OF COURSE, I HADN'T TAKEN PART IN THE UPRISING, AND MY NON-PARTICIPATION MIGHT HAVE COME ACROSS AS A SUBTLE STRATEGY."

BUT WHILE I WORKED FOR YOU REORGANIZING THE PARTY POLICE AFTER THE UPRISING WAS PUT DOWN...

"...LATER WHILE I STAYED BY YOUR SIDE IN MOSCOW, COMPLETING MY POLITICAL TRAINING...

"I OFTEN MUSED THAT IT WAS ONLY MY CHANCE DISCOVERY OF YOUR ASSOCIATE'S DEATH THAT CAUSED ME TO BECOME A REPLACEMENT FOR HIM."

DINNERTIME, GENTLEMEN!

TIBOR ILLYES 1891-1956

42

124

WE'RE GOING TO THE TABLE NOW, VASSILY ALEXANDROVICH.

SO *WHAT* WERE YOU TALKING TO HIM ABOUT THAT MADE HIM LOOK SO PENSIVE AND SERIOUS, JANOS?

I WAS TALKING ABOUT BUDAPEST, IN 1956.

UTTER *FOOLISHNESS*, YOUR "PEOPLE'S GLORIOUS UPRISING."

WELL, WELL, I THOUGHT IT WAS THE CZECHS THAT WERE "NAIVE AND PREMATURE?"

WHAT HAPPENED TO YOUR NEIGHBORS ALMOST TEN YEARS EARLIER SHOULD HAVE OPENED YOUR EYES, DON'T YOU THINK?

JUST A MOMENT, COMRADE NICOLESCU. IN '68 IT WAS OUR PARTY ITSELF, NOT THE SUBVERSIVE ELEMENTS, THAT WAS STRUGGLING TO REFORM SOCIALISM.

SUBVERSIVE? I ASK YOU, PAVEL, WHAT EXACTLY DO YOU MEAN BY SUBVERSIVE, EH? ANYWAY, THERE'S NO NEED FOR ME TO TIRE MYSELF OUT LIKE THIS.

INTERPRETER!

YES, COMRADE.

PLEASE, SIT DOWN!

KINDLY EXPLAIN IN THEIR RESPECTIVE BARBARIAN TONGUES WHAT I THINK OF OUR TWO ILL-INFORMED COMRADES AND THEIR NOTIONS OF HISTORY.

LOOK, JANOS, I'M HERE TO TRANSLATE, BUT--

BUT DON'T WORRY ABOUT IT! I'M SURE SERGEI SHAVANIDZE DOESN'T ENJOY THESE TYPES OF ARGUMENTS.

ACTUALLY, HE WISHES ME TO GIVE HIM THE GIST OF YOUR FASCINATING CONVERSATION.

NOT WORTH IT. HE'LL JUST LECTURE US AGAIN ABOUT OUR PETTY BOURGEOIS NATIONALISM.

WHAT SHALL I DO? DO...DO I TRANSLATE, OR--

COME UP WITH YOUR BEST FIGURES OF SPEECH, MY FRIEND.

AND MAKE SURE NOT TO SPOIL OUR ENJOYMENT OF THE CAVIAR FROM THE GREAT HOMELAND OF TRUE SOCIALISM, COURTESY OF SERGEI SHAVANIDZE, NEW BENEFACTOR TO US ALL.

LET'S DRINK A TOAST TO THE FATHERLAND OF THE REVOLUTION!

AND ITS TWO EMINENT REPRESENTATIVES, ALEXANDROVICH CHEVCHENKO AND SERGEI SHAVANIDZE!

AND ALSO TO ITS MARXIST STURGEON, BY GOD!

HA! HA! HA!

THIS WOULD TASTE EVEN BETTER WITH THE WHITE WINE ANNOUNCED ON THE MENU, WOULDN'T IT WAITER?

PROSZE PRZENIESC BIALE WINO?

DOBDRZE PROSZE PANA.

THESE POLES ARE STILL ALWAYS BUNGLING THINGS.

REALLY, GÜNTHER, CALM DOWN.

НЕ ХОТИТЕ ЛИ ВЫ ИГРАТЬ ШАШКИ, ВАСИЛИ АЛЕКСАНДРО-ВИЧ ?

BROOO...

LOOK...JUST LIKE ALWAYS, SERGEI SHAVANIDZE WANTS TO MATCH WITS WITH VASSILY ALEXANDROVICH AT CHESS.

AND LIKE *ALWAYS*...

HE'LL LOSE.

СПОКОЙНОЙ НОЧИ...

AND HE'S A VERY SORE LOSER.

COME ALONG, WE'RE ALL GOING TO GO TO BED NOW. TOMORROW IS A VERY BUSY DAY.

OUR ROOMS ARE RIGHT BESIDE VASSILY ALEXANDROVICH'S.

WHAT CAN HE BE THINKING?

PAH...

ABOUT THE PAST, SURELY.

"AS HE SO OFTEN DOES.

"BUT THERE ARE MANY PASTS, ALL INTERMINGLING...

"AND MANY PASTS, THAT SOMETIMES CONTRADICT EACH OTHER.

"THEN AGAIN, VASSILY ALEXANDROVICH ALWAYS REMAINS A MAN OF THE PRESENT.

OR PERHAPS HE'S EVEN THINKING AHEAD TO THE FUTURE, LIKE WE ALL DO?

"NOW, GOODNIGHT, MY BOY."
"GOODNIGHT, EVGENY."

46

IS EVERYONE FEELING WELL THIS MORNING?

PERFECTLY WELL.

ALL THE BETTER... VASSILY ALEXANDROVICH IS READY TO GO AND THE CARS ARE WAITING TO TAKE US TO THE WOODS.

IT'S STILL OVERCAST.

THAT WOULDN'T BE SO BAD FOR WHAT WE'RE PLANNING.

WHAT ARE WE PLANNING?

NOTHING, COMRADE, NOTHING. JUST TODAY'S UPCOMING HUNT, NOTHING MORE.

TODAY IT'S BOAR IN THE MORNING, THEN STAG IN THE AFTERNOON.

IS HE STILL UPSET ABOUT LOSING THE CHESS GAME LAST NIGHT?

NO, I DON'T THINK SO.

HE'S WHAT YOU MIGHT CALL A "MEAT FANATIC," JUST LIKE ONE OF YOUR FRENCH PRESIDENTS WAS, AND LOOK WHAT BAD LUCK IT BROUGHT HIM--

NOW HOLD ON THERE!

HE WASN'T MY PRESIDENT, ANY MORE THAN THE SOCIAL DEMOCRAT WHO TOOK HIS PLACE.

SPOKEN LIKE A YOUNG COMMUNIST WHO'S LEARNED HIS DOCTRINE *WELL.*

BESIDES, YOU YOURSELF SEEM TO BE DEVELOPING A TASTE FOR THIS CRUEL PURSUIT.

ME?!

JUST AN IMPRESSION... IT'S PART OF HUMAN NATURE, AS THE BOURGEOIS PHILOSOPHERS SAY.

YOU MOCK ME, *TADEUSZ.*

IT'S JUST THAT I--

LET'S DROP IT, SHALL WE? AND WE'LL SAY THAT SERGEI SHAVANIDZE HUNTS FOR THE SAKE OF MAKING HIS OWN KILLS. THAT'S ALL.

NOT AT ALL. IT'S JUST THAT I'VE SEEN TOO MANY PREDATORS IN MY LIFETIME. MY GOOD KARL AND JOSEF INCLUDED.

...

ТАК ... ХОРОШО ...

130

VICIOUS CREATURES, MY YOUNG FRENCH FRIEND, BELIEVE ME. AND THEY'VE GOT THEIR BLOOD UP THIS MORNING. I BELIEVE I'LL STAY RIGHT HERE.

I'M GOING TO GO ON A BIT FARTHER.

NA POMOC....!

YOU HEAR THAT? WHAT IS IT?

SOUNDS LIKE TADEUSZ'S VOICE.

AND IT SOUNDS LIKE HE'S IN TROUBLE!

I WAS WITH HIM NOT TOO LONG AGO.

FOLLOW ME!

I DON'T UNDERSTAND. NOTHING WAS SUPPOSED TO HAPPEN TODAY.

YES, IT IS STRANGE...

WAIT. NOW I'M NOT SO SURE WHERE...

I DON'T LIKE THIS.

ME NEITHER.

STILL, I'M CERTAIN THAT...

WHERE IS VASSILY ALEXANDROVICH, BY GOD?

I DON'T KNOW.

AND SHAVANIDZE?

ONE OF THE RANGERS TOLD ME HE'S FAR UP AHEAD. ON A KILLING SPREE.

ИДИТЕ СЮДО!

WHAT'S HE SAYING?

HE'S TELLING US TO FOLLOW HIM.

DID SOMETHING HAPPEN?

THAT'S WHAT WE'RE WONDERING.

OH LORD, WHAT NOW?

TOO RISKY TO SHOOT!

IT'S GOING TO CHARGE!

BLAM

WHO FIRED THAT SHOT?

IT WAS VASSILY ALEXANDROVICH!

WHAT AN *INCREDIBLE* SHOT!

WELL DONE, VASSILY!

YOU OKAY, TADEUSZ?

NOTHING SERIOUS, MY FRIENDS. BUT THAT WAS JUST IN TIME.

THIS CALLS FOR A DRINK! YOU SCARED US, YOU IDIOT! WE THOUGHT THE PLANS HAD BEEN CHANGED, AND--

SHUT YOUR MOUTH! YOU'RE THE IDIOT!

ЧТО СЛУЧИЛОСЬ ?

EXPLAIN TO HIM WHAT HAPPENED.

ОН РАНЕН?

ДА, ЭТО КАБАН ...

...ЭТОГО СЛЕДОВАЛО ОЖИДАТЬ...

SERGEI SHAVANIDZE SAYS THAT IT WAS BOUND TO HAPPEN, YOU DON'T GO WALKING AROUND UNARMED WHEN THERE'S A HUNT ON.

OH YEAH? WELL YOU JUST TELL HIM THAT.

YOU JUST TELL HIM NOTHING! WE'RE RIGHT NEAR THE HUNTING LODGE, WHERE LUNCH IS WAITING FOR US.

I'LL GET MY WOUNDS BANDAGED THERE WHILE WE DRINK A TOAST TO VASSILY ALEXANDROVICH, WHO HAS JUST GRANTED ME MY THIRD LIFE!

YOUR *THIRD* LIFE? WHAT ARE YOU TALKING ABOUT?

OH, IT'S A LONG STORY, AND SOME OF YOU KNOW FRAGMENTS OF IT, AT LEAST...FOR I OWE THREE LIVES BUT *ALSO* THREE DEATHS TO VASSILY ALEXANDROVICH.

"THE FIRST LIFE I OWE HIM HAPPENED WHEN HE CAME TO JOIN ME IN ODESSA IN 1938, WHILE I WAS RECOVERING FROM A SERIOUS WOUND INFLICTED BY THE POLISH POLICE AS I WAS ESCAPING JUSTICE.

52

"OUR PARTY HAD JUST BEEN DISSOLVED BY THE COMINTERN, SUPPOSEDLY FOR TROTSKYISM, AND A HUNDRED OF ITS LEADERS WERE LIQUIDATED IN MOSCOW.

I SHOULD HAVE BEEN AMONG THEM.

"BUT BECAUSE, DESPITE EVERYTHING, HE WAS THINKING OF THE FUTURE, VASSILY ALEXANDROVICH SHIPPED ME OUT ON A LEAKY OLD TUB ACROSS THE BLACK SEA TO ISTANBUL.

BY THE TIME THE FIRST GERMAN BOMBS FELL ON WARSAW IN SEPTEMBER 1939, I HAD RETURNED *SECRETLY*, AT HIS REQUEST.

"BUT I HAD CHOSEN TO LIVE WITH MY PEOPLE, AS A JEW AS WELL AS A COMMUNIST. THEN THE NAZIS' EXTERMINATION OF THE 'UNTERMENSCHEN' BEGAN.

53

135

"THE GHETTO! FIVE HUNDRED THOUSAND PEOPLE... THERE WOULD ONLY BE TWO HUNDRED SURVIVORS, MYSELF AMONG THEM.

"CHILDREN ROASTED IN FIRES STARTED B[Y] FLAMETHROWERS. PARENTS MURDERIN[G] THEIR CHILDREN TO SPARE THEM THE HORROR.

IN 1943, AT THE TIME OF THE GHETTO UPRISING, WHILE THE S.S. WAS BLOWING EVERYTHING UP WITH DYNAMITE, IT WAS THROUGH ANOTHER INTERVENTION BY VASSILY ALEXANDROVICH THAT MY ESCAPE WAS PLANNED. THE LEADERLESS PARTY HAD TO BE REFORMED AND THEY WANTED ME *ALIVE* RATHER THAN DEAD.

"CORPSES CARTED AWAY DAILY IN BARROWS, THE SMELL OF DEAD FLESH PREVAILING IN THE RUINED CITY, I LIVED THROUGH IT ALL.

"AFTER THE WAR, I WALKED WITH HIM THROUGH THE IMMENSE SLAUGHTERHOUSE REEKING OF ROTTING BODIES FROM UNDER THE RUBBLE. FULL OF PASSION, I DREAMED OF THE RECONSTRUCTION OF MY RAVAGED NATION.

SK

"AND FINALLY TODAY, AS YOU ALL SAW..."

"VASSILY ALEXANDROVICH ONCE AGAIN RENEWED MY PERMIT TO LIVE ON THIS EARTH."

HERE'S TO THE THREE LIVES I OWE HIM!

AND THE THREE DEATHS?

"THE FIRST ONE HAPPENED IN ODESSA WHEN I, A YOUNG JEW FROM WILNO, VERY PASSIONATE ABOUT THE REGIME, FIRST LOST FAITH IN THE HOMELAND OF SOCIALISM, RELENTLESS IN ITS OBLITERATION OF THE MOST DEVOTED COMMUNIST MILITANTS IN OTHER COUNTRIES."

"THE SECOND GOES BACK TO THE END OF THE WAR."

"I HAD BECOME A RANKING MEMBER OF WARSAW'S POLITBURO, AND, AMONG MANY OTHER DUTIES, I WAS IN CHARGE OF OVERSEEING THE CONSTRUCTION OF A CULTURAL CENTER BEQUEATHED UPON THE MARTYRED POLISH PEOPLE BY THEIR SOVIET BRETHREN."

"I QUICKLY REALIZED THE PRICE THAT HAD TO BE PAID TO OUR GENEROUS, BUT DEMANDING PROTECTOR, TO OUR 'BIG BROTHER,' SO SURE OF HIMSELF, SO RIGID, TO THE CRUEL OGRE THAT DEVOURED ITS OWN CHILDREN... THAT WAS WHEN I KNEW SHAME."

55

"BUT IT WASN'T UNTIL 1967, UNTIL MY THIRD DEATH, MY POLITICAL DEATH, THAT I REALLY UNDERSTOOD. IT WAS VASSILY ALEXANDROVICH HIMSELF WHO CAME TO GIVE ME THE NEWS IN THE SAME CULTURAL CENTER THAT I MYSELF HELPED BUILD.

"THE REGIME NEEDED SCAPEGOATS TO ACCOUNT FOR ITS FAILINGS. AND WHO DID THEY PICK, MIGHT I ASK? THOSE RARE JEWS WHO HAD ESCAPED THE GERMAN GENOCIDE, SYSTEMATIC AS IT WAS...

"OUTSIDE, PEOPLE WERE SHOUTING DOWN WITH THE 'MOSZKI DO PALESTINY'--'THE MOSESES OF PALESTINE.' AND I, TADEUSZ BOCZEK, WAS DISMISSED, ALTHOUGH THANKS TO THE INTERVENTION OF VASSILY ALEXANDROVICH, I WAS FORTUNATE ENOUGH TO BE WHISKED AWAY TO THIS FAR-OFF COUNTRY.

THAT'S THE STORY OF MY THREE LIVES AND MY THREE DEATHS, MY FRIENDS.

SERGEI SHAVANIDZE IS ONLY HALF-SURPRISED AT THE *CONSISTENTLY* ANTI-SOVIET TONE OF MR. BOCZEK'S REMARKS.

AND HE POINTS OUT THAT VASSILY ALEXANDROVICH NEVER DID HAVE GOOD LUCK WITH HIS MEN IN WARSAW.

VERY TRUE.

SPEAKING OF WHICH, WHAT BECAME OF THE BRIGHT YOUNG KAZIMIR DUNECKI WHO TOOK OVER FROM YOU, TADEUSZ?

ALAS, MY DEAR GÜNTHER, HE WASN'T QUITE BRIGHT ENOUGH. HE WAS OVERWHELMED BY SOLIDARNOSO ALONG WITH ALL THE OTHERS, AS YOU KNOW VERY WELL.

AND I EVEN HEARD A REPORT AFTER I RETIRED THAT HE HAD LEFT THE COUNTRY TO UNDERGO TREATMENT AT A CLINIC SOMEWHERE NEAR MOSCOW.

BUT UNDOUBTEDLY OUR COMRADE SERGEI SHAVANIDZE KNOWS *MORE* THAN I DO ABOUT THAT, RIGHT?

ПАН БОЦЕК, СПРОШИВАЕТ ГДЕ СЕЙЧАС НАХОДИТСЯ ПАН ДУНЕЦК ...

... Я НИЧЕГО НЕ МОГУ СКАЗАТЬ ПО ЭТОМУ ПОВО-ДУ ...

MR. SHAVANIDZE HAS NO COMMENT TO MAKE ON THAT SUBJECT, AND IN ANY CASE HE THOROUGHLY *DISAPPROVES* OF THE MANNER IN WHICH THE U.P.W.P. DEALT WITH THE OVERT CRISIS CAUSED BY THE ANTI-SOCIALIST AND ANTI-SOVIET ELEMENTS FROM VARIOUS MINOR GROUPS.

HMM...THEN I TOO AM ONLY HALF-SURPRISED AT HIS OPINIONS.

LET'S DROP IT, AND *ENJOY* OURSELVES!

GOOD IDEA. ANYWAY, THE WEATHER'S GETTING COLD, AND WE'D BETTER GET GOING.

I'LL WAIT FOR YOU *HERE!* I'VE HAD ENOUGH EXCITEMENT FOR ONE DAY.

THEN WE'LL SEE YOU SOON, TADEUSZ!

JUST WOUNDED, MY BOY. THE RANGERS WILL HAVE TO FINISH IT OFF!

I'M SO SORRY.

WELL?

ПРЕКРАСНОЕ
...

SERGEI SHAVANIDZE IS *VERY* PLEASED.

MUCH THE BETTER. AND NOW, WE CAN RETURN.

NIGHT IS FALLING...

AND IT'S GOING TO BE A COLD ONE.

NO MATTER, OUR ACCOMMODATIONS ARE COZY.

YES, AND A QUICK STOP AT THE BAR OUGHT TO LIFT OUR SPIRITS!

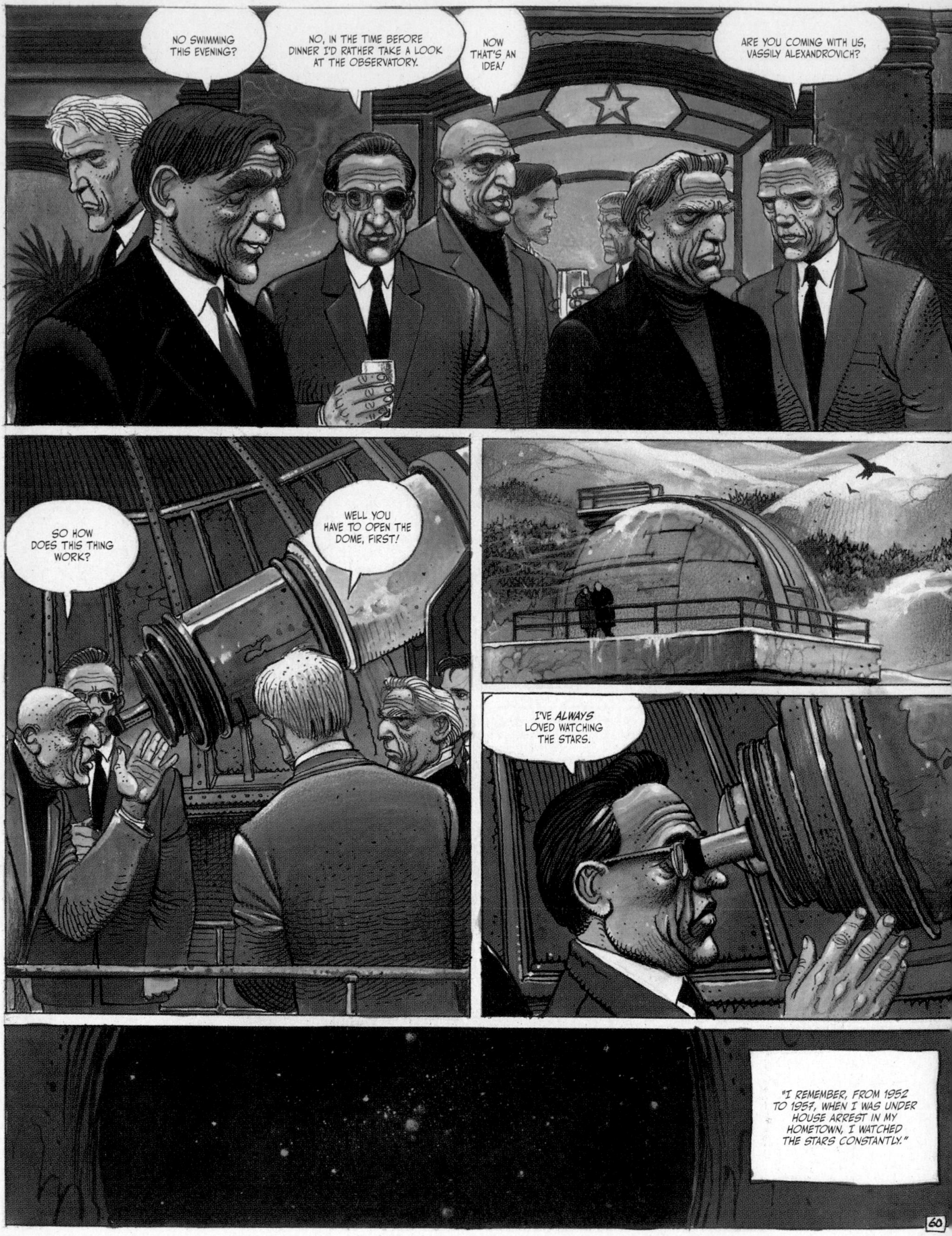
NO SWIMMING THIS EVENING?
NO, IN THE TIME BEFORE DINNER I'D RATHER TAKE A LOOK AT THE OBSERVATORY.
NOW THAT'S AN IDEA!
ARE YOU COMING WITH US, VASSILY ALEXANDROVICH?
SO HOW DOES THIS THING WORK?
WELL YOU HAVE TO OPEN THE DOME, FIRST!
I'VE *ALWAYS* LOVED WATCHING THE STARS.
"I REMEMBER, FROM 1952 TO 1957, WHEN I WAS UNDER HOUSE ARREST IN MY HOMETOWN, I WATCHED THE STARS CONSTANTLY."
60

WAS THAT WHEN YOU HAD FALLEN FROM FAVOR, *DESPITE* YOUR ROLE IN THE SECURITATE DURING THE PURGES?

THAT'S RIGHT, EVGENY. THE SAME TIME THAT ANA PAUKNER, THE RED TIGRESS, WAS STRIPPED OF HER FOREIGN AFFAIRS DUTIES...

DON'T WORRY ABOUT IT, COMRADE NICOLESCU. IT'S NOT MUCH OF AN HONOR TO BE A MEMBER OF THE POLITICAL POLICE IN A COUNTRY THAT CONSTITUTES A KEY PART OF "THE SOVIET STRONGHOLD," AS WE CALL IT.

MAYBE NOT.

LET'S JUST SAY THAT'S HOW WE *LEARNED* TO BE CAUTIOUS, US ROMANIANS.

OH, THANKS. THAT'S A *SLAP* IN THE FACE TO US HUNGARIANS.

COMING THROUGH LOUD AND CLEAR ON THE CZECH SIDE TOO, BUDDY.

ALL YOUR POLITICAL TAUNTS ARE DRIVING ME CRAZY!

"AS I WAS SAYING, I OFTEN WATCHED THE SKY, BY MY MOTHER'S SIDE."

"AND DESPITE MY MISFORTUNES, A RECURRENT DREAM FROM MY YOUTH KEPT COMING BACK TO ME. I HAD IT FOR THE FIRST TIME IN 1945, ON THE RETURN TRIP FROM RUSSIA WITH GEORGHIU-DEJ'S GROUP."

"AT THAT TIME, I EVEN TOLD IT TO VASSILY ALEXANDROVICH, WHO WAS RETURNING TO BUCHAREST WITH US IN ORDER TO RESTORE ORDER IN THE COUNTRY, AFTER THE YALTA CONFERENCE."

"I SAW MYSELF AS A STORK, THE BIRD OF FORTUNE AND FERTILITY, ARRIVING ABOVE MY VILLAGE WITH ITS COLORFUL COTTAGES.

"OR SOMETIMES AS A PELICAN, FULL OF WISDOM AND GENEROSITY, LIKE THOSE THAT LIVE IN THE DANUBE DELTA AND FISH FOR THEIR VERY POOR MASTERS.

"OR EVEN AS A POWERFUL, UNNAMED BIRD, BEARING A MESSAGE OF STRENGTH AND JUSTICE ON ITS WAY THROUGH THE ETHER.

"AND THROUGHOU MY HOUSE ARRES BEFORE VASSILY ALEXANDROVICH CAME BACK TO LOOK FOR ME, I WANTED AT ALL COSTS TO HAVE THAT DREAM AGAI!"

AFTER THAT, DID YOU HAVE IT AGAIN ALONG YOUR NUMEROUS TRAVELS SPREADING THE GOOD WORD FOR ROMANIAN DIPLOMACY?

SOMETIMES, VASIL, SOMETIMES...

AND ALSO WHILE YOU WERE DOZING THROUGH CENTRAL COMMITTEE MEETINGS?

AHEM...

WELL, YOU WERE *LUCKY* TO HAVE SUCH A DREAM, ION NICOLESCU.

"BECAUSE I NEVER DREAM OF THE TIME THAT I WAS A PARTISAN LEADER OF THE FIRST UNDERGROUND FORCES IN THE RHODOPE MOUNTAINS.

"NOR OF THE TIME WHEN I FORMED PART OF THE FIRST DIMITROV ADMINISTRATION, WITH VASSILY ALEXANDROVICH'S BLESSING.

"IT TOOK MY NEAR ESCAPE FROM HANGING, ON THE APPARENT CHARGE OF TITOISM, TO START ME DREAMING."

AND ALTHOUGH VASSILY ALEXANDROVICH SAVED MY REPUTATION BY APPOINTING ME THE ARCHITECT OF THE BULGARIAN PEASANTRY'S "GREAT LEAP FORWARD," AS WE CALLED IT IN '58...

"I'VE HAD THE SAME NIGHTMARE EVER SINCE.

"A SHAPELESS AND OBSCENE MONSTER COMES FROM, I DON'T KNOW WHAT COLD AND FROZEN PLANET...

"AND IT OCCURS TO ME THAT THIS MONSTER MIGHT BE ME, VASIL STROYANOV, OR ELSE IT'S THE PARTY ITSELF, AND I'M JUST ITS FOUL MOUTH, OR ONE HORRIBLE CLAW."

OH, COME NOW! YOU'VE JUST HAD TOO MUCH TO DRINK SINCE ATTENDING TO YOUR DUTIES FOR THE FATHERLAND FRONT, EVEN THOUGH THEY'RE ONLY HONORARY ONES.

IT WOULD BE EASIER TO PUT HIS REMARKS DOWN TO SIMPLE DELIRIUM.

OH, I DIDN'T SEE YOU THERE, GÜNTHER.

YES, AND I'VE BEEN LISTENING TO YOUR RAMBLINGS FOR SOME TIME.

AND?

AND I MUST SAY I DON'T HAVE ANY REGRETS ABOUT SPEAKING OUT, AT THE APPROPRIATE TIME, AGAINST REHABILITATING KAFKA.

BECAUSE I ALWAYS KNEW THAT HE WAS NOTHING BUT A BOURGEOIS AUTHOR, CORRODED BY PESSIMISM.

BUT I WOULD NEVER HAVE BELIEVED THAT FORMER HEROES OF THE REVOLUTION LIKE YOURSELVES WOULD BE CAPABLE OF SUCH CHILDISH IDEALISM.

PARDON ME FOR INTERRUPTING YOUR DISTINGUISHED LITERARY CONVERSATION, MY REFINED FRIENDS...

...BUT IT'S TIME TO ENJOY SOME GOOD FOOD!

ANYTHING'S BETTER THAN LISTENING TO THIS NONSENSE.

GÜNTHER'S BECOME MORE AND MORE FANATICAL EVER SINCE HE STARTED CONSORTING WITH SHAVANIDZE.

YES... YOU'RE RIGHT.

HE'S BECOME THE MOUTHPIECE FOR HIS NEW MASTER. WHICH IS DANGEROUS, CONSIDERING OUR PLANS.

KEEP QUIET, NICOLESCU! WE ALL KNOW THE SCORE WITH GÜNTHER. NO POINT GOING OVER EVERYTHING AGAIN, IT'S ALL BEEN ARRANGED.

YOU'RE RIGHT. LET'S EAT WITH LIGHT HEARTS.

AND DRINK TILL WE'RE LIGHTHEADED!

НА ЗДОРОВЛЕ!

HIC...

СПОСИБО... СПОКОЙНОЙ НОЧИ...

147

THAT'S IT. HE LOST *AGAIN*.

WELL, I'D SAY HE'S *DEFINITELY* ANGRY ABOUT IT.

GOOD NIGHT. HAVE PLEASANT DREAMS.

I DON'T THINK I CAN MANAGE THAT...

WHO CAN?

66

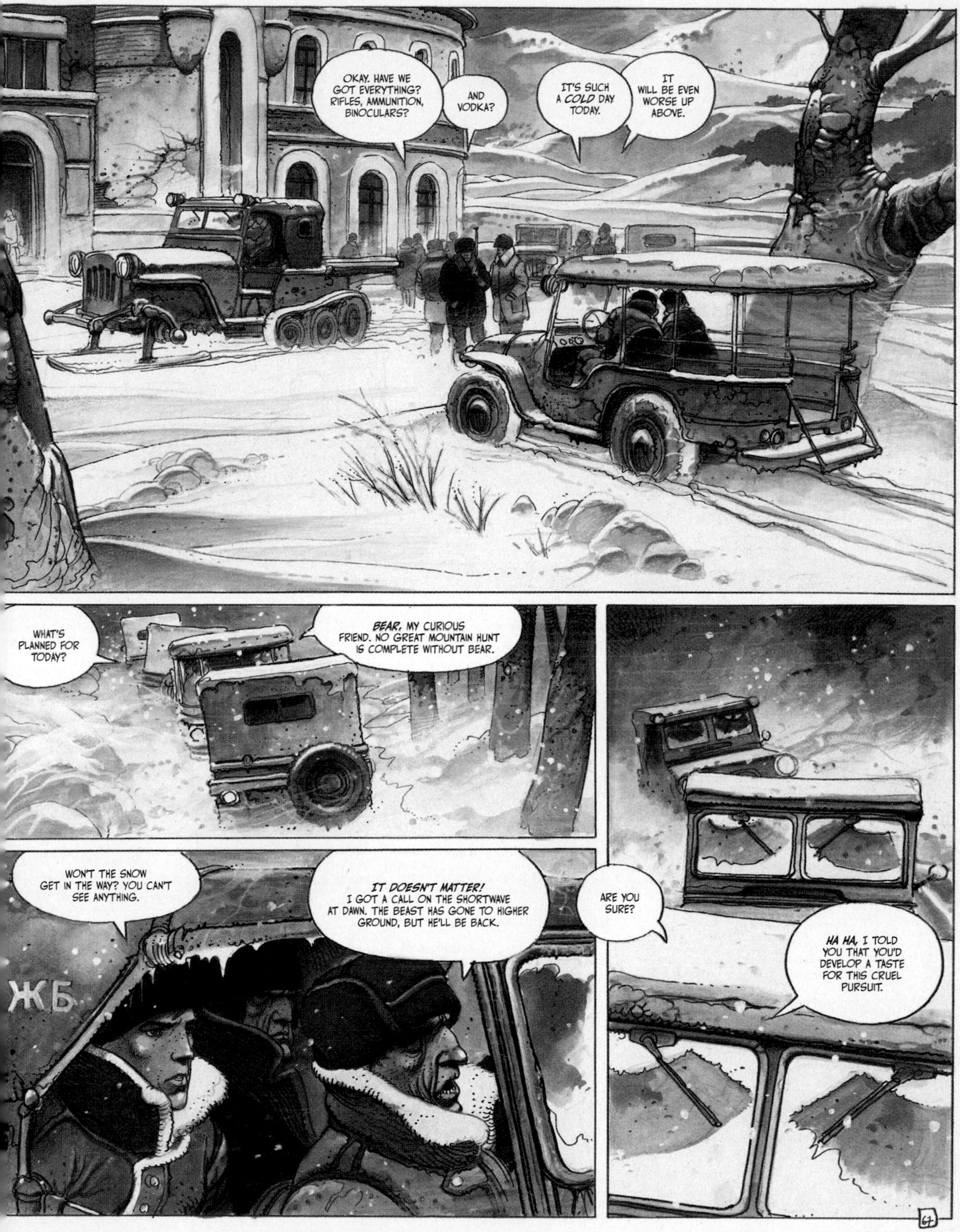

OKAY. HAVE WE GOT EVERYTHING? RIFLES, AMMUNITION, BINOCULARS?
AND VODKA?
IT'S SUCH A *COLD* DAY TODAY.
IT WILL BE EVEN WORSE UP ABOVE.
WHAT'S PLANNED FOR TODAY?
BEAR, MY CURIOUS FRIEND. NO GREAT MOUNTAIN HUNT IS COMPLETE WITHOUT BEAR.
WON'T THE SNOW GET IN THE WAY? YOU CAN'T SEE ANYTHING.
IT DOESN'T MATTER! I GOT A CALL ON THE SHORTWAVE AT DAWN. THE BEAST HAS GONE TO HIGHER GROUND, BUT HE'LL BE BACK.
ЖБ
ARE YOU SURE?
HA HA, I TOLD YOU THAT YOU'D DEVELOP A TASTE FOR THIS CRUEL PURSUIT.
67

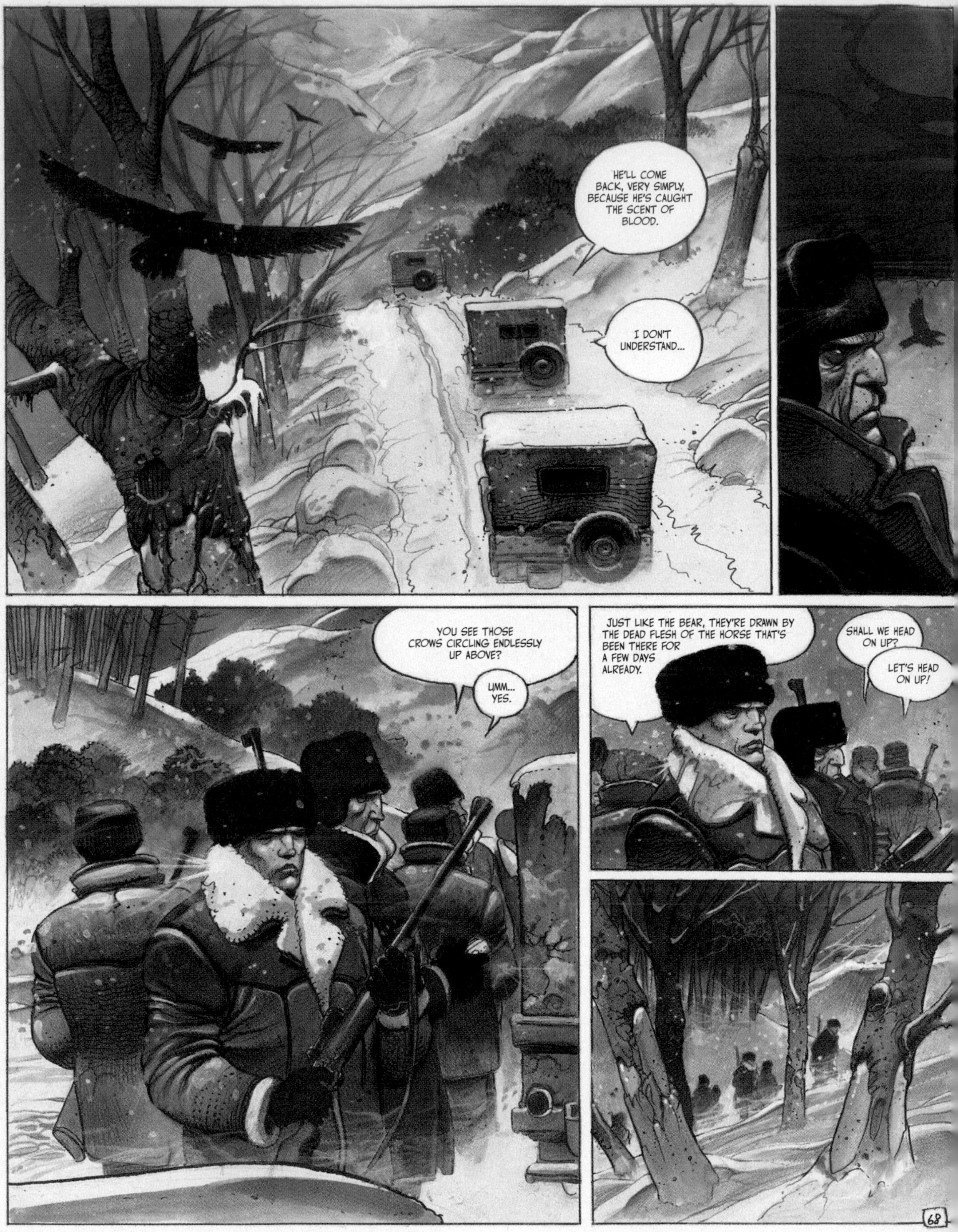

HE'LL COME BACK, VERY SIMPLY, BECAUSE HE'S CAUGHT THE SCENT OF BLOOD.
I DON'T UNDERSTAND...
YOU SEE THOSE CROWS CIRCLING ENDLESSLY UP ABOVE?
UMM... YES.
JUST LIKE THE BEAR, THEY'RE DRAWN BY THE DEAD FLESH OF THE HORSE THAT'S BEEN THERE FOR A FEW DAYS ALREADY.
SHALL WE HEAD ON UP?
LET'S HEAD ON UP!
68

ROTTING FLESH... IT'S *HORRIBLE.*

COME ON, JANOS, NO LAST MINUTE SQUEAMISHNESS!

WHAT IS HE DOING?

VASSILY ALEXANDROVICH IS ASSIGNING OUR POSTS FOR THE HUNT.

ONCE IN POSITION, *NOBODY* CAN MOVE...FOR ANY REASON.

ALL RIGHT! LISTEN, EVERYBODY!

JANOS AND PAVEL, BEHIND THOSE ROCKS DOWN THERE!

VASIL AND ION, OVER THERE IN THAT THICKET!

SERGEI, IN THE GORGE. ALONE, LIKE YOU PREFER.

ПЕРЕ-ВОДУ ВАМ...
...

SERGEI SHAVANIDZE ISN'T SATISFIED WITH HIS POSITION. HE SAYS HE WON'T HAVE A CHANCE OF SPOTTING THE BEAR.

GÜNTHER AND VASSILY ALEXANDROVICH, EACH ON ONE SIDE OF THE HILL.

LIMM... EXCUSE ME.

TOO LATE TO ARGUE!
HE KNOWS VERY WELL WE HAVE TO GET GOING RIGHT NOW!!!

HE'S UPSET.

DON'T WORRY SO MUCH ALL THE TIME ABOUT HIS MOODS, AND COME THIS WAY. THE BEAR SHOULDN'T BE LONG IN COMING.

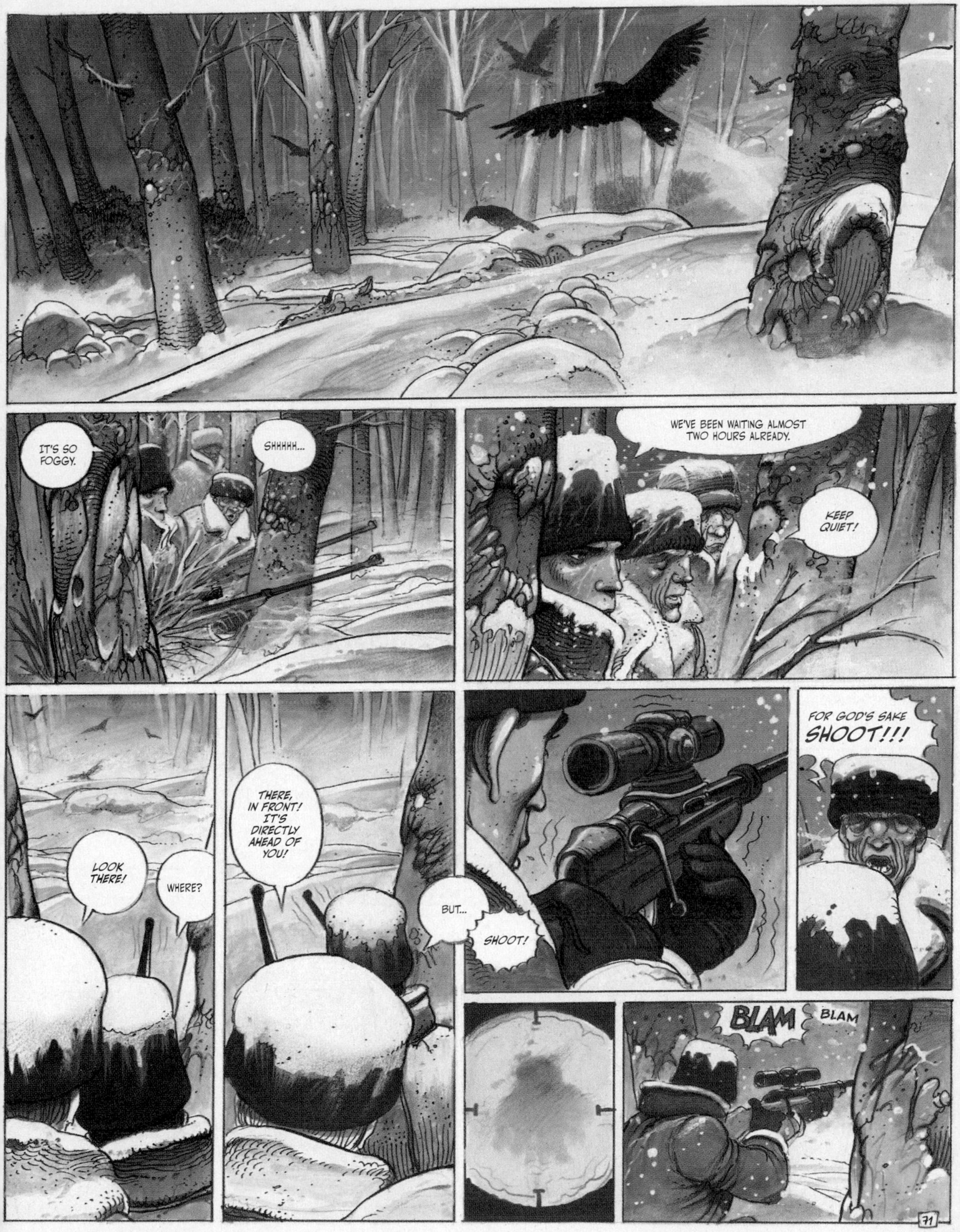
IT'S SO FOGGY.
SHHHHH...
WE'VE BEEN WAITING ALMOST TWO HOURS ALREADY.
KEEP QUIET!
LOOK THERE!
WHERE?
THERE, IN FRONT! IT'S DIRECTLY AHEAD OF YOU!
BUT...
SHOOT!
FOR GOD'S SAKE SHOOT!!!
BLAM
BLAM
71

GREAT!!! YOU GOT HIM!

Y-YOU THINK SO?

FOLLOW US!

OH SHIT! IT'S SHAVANIDZE!

WHY'D THE CRAZY BASTARD COME BACK DOWN?!

WHAT'S GOING ON?

IT-IT WASN'T ME! THERE WAS ANOTHER GUNSHOT! I--

ANOTHER GUNSHOT? YOU WISH IT WAS, YOU DUMB KID! THAT WAS THE ECHO!

WHAT HAVE YOU DONE, YOU BUNCH OF BASTARDS?! WHAT HAVE YOU DONE!?

IT WAS AN ACCIDENT, GÜNTHER. A TRAGIC ACCIDENT.

AN ACCIDENT?!!? YOU BAND OF ANTI-PARTY TRAITORS. YOU KNOW VERY WELL IT WAS A POLITICAL ASSASSINATION!

HEY, JUST CALM DOWN THERE, MR. GÜNTHER-KNOW-IT-ALL! IT SEEMS TO ME THAT SERGEI SHAVANIDZE DIDN'T FOLLOW VASSILY ALEXANDROVICH'S INSTRUCTIONS, AND--

ENOUGH OF YOUR BULLSHIT, VASIL!!!

IT WAS ALL PREARRANGED! YOU ASSIGNED HIM A BAD POST KNOWING FULL WELL THAT HE WOULDN'T STAY THERE, AND THIS YOUNG FRENCH IDIOT WAS SHAMELESSLY MANIPULATED TO--

ME? BUT...I-I ASSURE YOU THAT--

I'LL DENOUNCE EVERY ONE OF YOU! DON'T COUNT ON MY FORMER FRIENDSHIP TO COVER UP THIS FILTHY MURDER!!!

DON'T COUNT ON OURS EITHER, GÜNTHER!

DON'T COUNT ON IT AT ALL.

155

TWO HUNTING ACCIDENTS IN A ROW *OFTEN* HAPPEN...IN ALL THE CONFUSION.

VERY *OFTEN*...

GOOD GOD! WE FORGOT ALL ABOUT THE BEAR!

A MAGNIFICENT ANIMAL! ANYWAY WHO SHOT IT?

VASSILY ALEXANDROVICH, OF COURSE. A SHOT LIKE THAT...

GHASTLY... IT WAS THE SCENT OF HUMAN BLOOD THAT ATTRACTED IT.

I'VE ALREADY TOLD YOU, JANOS. NO LAST MINUTE SQUEAMISHNESS.

LISTEN, THE COPS AND THE RANGERS ARE ON THEIR WAY UP! YOU ALL KNOW YOUR PART, RIGHT?

I'M WARNING YOU, VASSILY ALEXANDROVICH, I DON'T KNOW, AND I REFUSE TO KNOW!

ME NEITHER, I-I DON'T KNOW WHAT...

YOU HAD *NO PART* IN ALL OF THIS. WE'LL EXPLAIN IT TO THEM.

BUT, GÜNTHER?

GÜNTHER WON'T SAY ANYTHING AND NEITHER WILL THE POLICE. VASSILY ALEXANDROVICH'S WORD IS THE *LAW* IN THESE PARTS, AND IN MANY OTHER PLACES TOO.

YOU SEE? VASSILY ALEXANDROVICH KNOWS TOO MUCH ABOUT HIM.

OKAY, WE'LL CLEAR OFF NOW. HAVE THEM BRING THE BODY. AND THE BEAR TOO, OF COURSE!

БОЖЕ МОЙ!

BEST GAME WE EVER BAGGED, *HA HA HA...*

SPARE US YOUR GALLOWS HUMOR, VASIL, PLEASE.

I'M IN A HURRY TO LEAVE. WITH ALL THIS SNOW I'M AFRAID THAT MY OLD TATRA WON'T MAKE IT TO PRAGUE.

AND I WISH I WERE ALREADY IN BUDAPEST.

HMM...THIS NEWS WILL CREATE AN UPROAR EVERYWHERE. WE'LL HAVE TO TURN IT TO OUR ADVANTAGE QUICKLY.

DON'T WORRY, MY FRIENDS. I'VE GIVEN THE ORDER TO HAVE YOUR BAGS PACKED, AND SPECIAL TRAIN SERVICES ARE WAITING.

SO WE'LL DROP OFF PAVEL AND THEN HEAD TO THE STATION.

THAT'S WHAT WAS PLANNED, JANOS. AS FOR THE BODY, IT WILL TRAVEL WITH VASSILY ALEXANDROVICH.

ALL VERY *LOGICAL,* TADEUSZ.

GET THE BAGS INTO THE CARS! WE'RE LEAVING!

FAREWELL, VASSILY ALEXANDROVICH. I HOPE WE'LL SEE EACH OTHER AGAIN.

IS THAT CAR COMING OR NOT?!

SEE YOU ALL LATER, COMRADES!

SEE YOU, PAVEL!

AND BE CAREFUL.

RIDE WITH US, GÜNTHER. YOU'LL FREEZE TO DEATH OUT THERE.

NO! I'LL STAY WITH HIM!

I DON'T UNDERSTAND, EVGENY, I REALLY DON'T UNDERSTAND. DID YOU BRING ME HERE ONLY TO DO... TO DO THAT? ALL YOU NEEDED WAS SOME FOOL TO *MANIPULATE?*

AH...

BUT WHY? ASSASSINATION IS...IS A FASCIST METHOD! COMMUNISM HAS ITS WHOLE FUTURE AHEAD OF IT! WHY RESORT TO UNDERHANDED TACTICS LIKE A STAGED HUNTING ACCIDENT?

OH, COME ON.

"TRY A BIT HARDER COMRADE. ALL THE MEN YOU JUST MET DON'T REPRESENT ONLY THEMSELVES."

EXACTLY! HISTORY ISN'T MADE BY INDIVIDUALS! IT'S THE MASSES THAT COUNT!

HAH, THE MASSES! DON'T MAKE ME LAUGH! IF VASSILY ALEXANDROVICH AND THE OLD MILITANTS YOU SAW WITH HIM THOUGHT IT NECESSARY TO PUT AN END TO THE ACTIVITIES OF THE NEW HEAD OF INTER-PARTY RELATIONS, IT'S BECAUSE THE MASSES WOULDN'T BE ABLE TO DO IT FOR THEMSELVES!

I REALLY DON'T UNDERSTAND...

77

"THEN YOU'RE AS NAIVE AS EVER. YOU SEE, VASSILY ALEXANDROVICH LOST HIS NAIVETÉ A LONG TIME AGO..."

"WITH THE DEATH OF VERA NIKOLAEVNA TRETIAKOVA PERHAPS?"

CONTRARY TO WHAT YOU BELIEVE, THIS LAST POLITICAL ACT IS THE ACT OF A *GREAT* MARXIST. IT'S THE ACT OF A MAN WHO BELIEVES IN THE REVERSIBILITY OF HISTORY.

I DON'T--

"I KNOW...YOU DON'T UNDERSTAND. BUT JUST TRY! DON'T YOU SEE THAT VASSILY ALEXANDROVICH, PRECISELY BECAUSE HE'S ALWAYS THINKING OF THE MASSES AND THEIR SUFFERING, BECAME AWARE OF THE DANGEROUS STAGNATION THAT HIS OWN ACTIONS AND THOSE OF MANY OTHERS WERE INFLICTING ON THE EASTERN BLOC NATIONS."

"AND BEFORE DYING HE WANTED TO LIFT THE LID, THE LID THAT SERGEI SHAVANIDZE WOULD HAVE KEPT HERMETICALLY SEALED IN THE NAME OF MOTHER RUSSIA'S INTERESTS."

EVGENY, HOW CAN YOU TALK THAT WAY ABOUT YOUR HOMELAND? ABOUT THE HOMELAND OF SOCIALISM?!!

I DON'T CARE ABOUT MY HOMELAND. I'M A TRUE INTERNATIONALIST, LIKE VASSILY ALEXANDROVICH. AND I WANT THE POPULAR DEMOCRACIES TO BE ABLE TO SET THEIR OWN PATH.

IF THERE'S STILL TIME.

YOU'RE ALL CRAZY!

NOT AT ALL, WE'RE NOT CRAZY! JUST THE OPPOSITE...WE'RE FULL OF *HOPE*.

AND WHAT ABOUT HOPE FOR ME, NOW? DID YOU THINK OF THAT?

AHEM...YOU'LL HAVE TO STAY IN MOSCOW A BIT LONGER THAN YOU PLANNED, LONG ENOUGH FOR THINGS TO SETTLE DOWN.

"AND YOU'LL HAVE TO LEARN TO LIVE WITH A BLOODY SECRET, LIKE SO MANY OF US.

"YOU DON'T HAVE ANYTHING TO WORRY ABOUT, IN FACT, BECAUSE AS FAR AS YOU'RE CONCERNED IT REALLY WAS AN ACCIDENT. WE TOOK ALL THE NECESSARY PRECAUTIONS."

EVERYTHING'S PROCEEDING PERFECTLY WELL, COMRADES. I ALREADY TELEPHONED OUR OLD FRIENDS IN WARSAW TO LET THEM KNOW ABOUT THE...UH...DEMISE. THEY'RE TERRIBLY SORRY, OF COURSE.

IN ANY CASE, WE ALL KNOW WHO'S GOING TO BE THE NEXT HEAD OF INTER-PARTY RELATIONS IN THE CENTRAL COMMITTEE. RIGHT, EVGENY GOLOZOV? MY *SINCERE* CONGRATULATIONS.

THE UNFORTUNATE SHAVANIDZE AFFAIR IS NOW CLOSED. *FAREWELL* TO THE LIVING.

AND TO THE DEAD.

GOODBYE, VASSILY ALEXANDROVICH.

TAKE CARE OF YOURSELF, LITTLE FATHER.

WE'LL DO THE SAME FOR OURSELVES.

AND THE FRENCHMAN?

DEPORTED! HE NEVER FOUND OUT ANYTHING, AND NEITHER DID THE LOCAL POLICE.

I DON'T KNOW IF WE'LL SEE EACH OTHER AGAIN, VASSILY ALEXANDROVICH, BUT I THANK YOU FOR GIVING ME THE CHANCE TO SERVE THE CAUSE OF SOCIALISM ONCE MORE.

YES, AND THANKS AGAIN FOR MY THIRD AND FINAL LIFE. *GOODBYE.*

OKAY, LET'S GO! THEY'RE WAITING FOR ME IN MOSCOW!

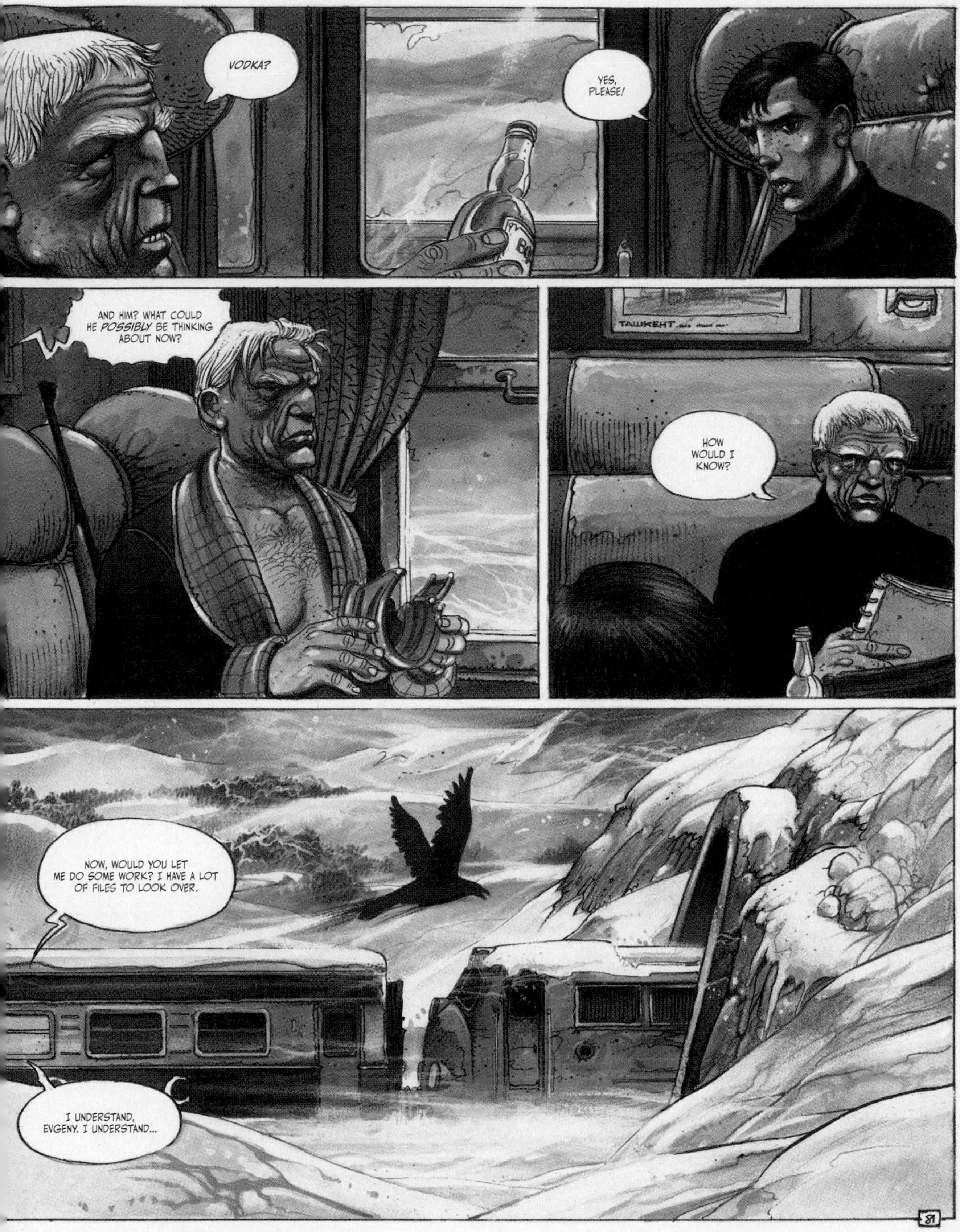
VODKA?
YES, PLEASE!
AND HIM? WHAT COULD HE POSSIBLY BE THINKING ABOUT NOW?
ТАШКЕНТ
HOW WOULD I KNOW?
NOW, WOULD YOU LET ME DO SOME WORK? I HAVE A LOT OF FILES TO LOOK OVER.
I UNDERSTAND, EVGENY. I UNDERSTAND...

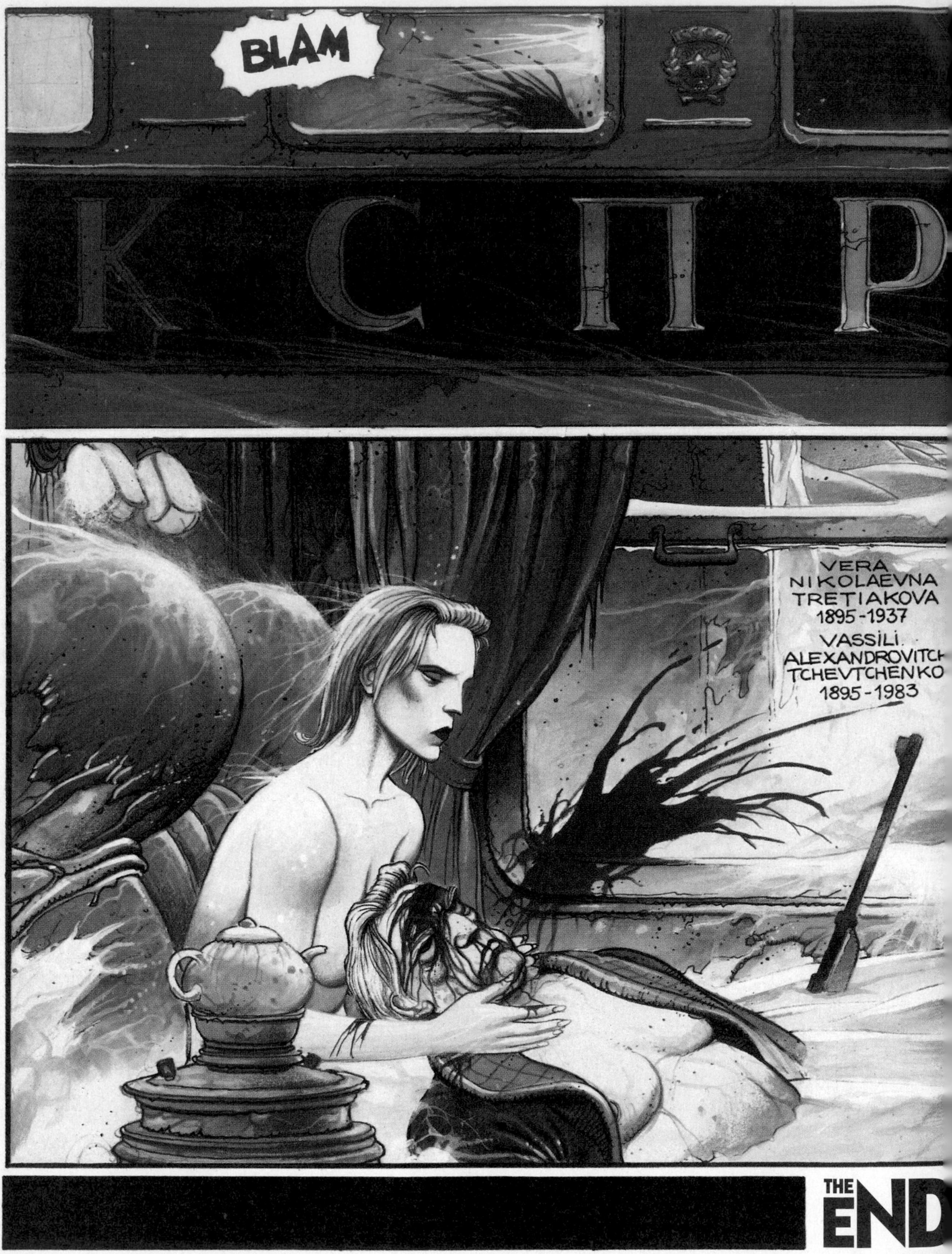
BLAM
КСПР
VERA NIKOLAEVNA TRETIAKOVA 1895-1937
VASSILI ALEXANDROVITCH TCHEVTCHENKO 1895-1983
THE END

COVER
GALLERY

¡NO PASARÁN!

ORIGINAL COVER FOR THE BLACK ORDER BRIGADE

ORIGINAL COVER FOR THE HUNTING PARTY

Look for these books from HUMANOIDS/DC COMICS:

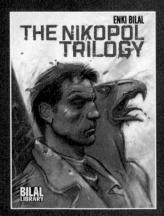  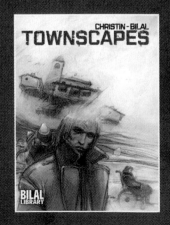